SUGAR SUGAR

Simon Bent

SUGAR SUGAR

OBERON BOOKS

LONDON

First published in 1998 by Oberon Books Ltd.
(incorporating Absolute Classics),
521 Caledonian Road, London N7 9RH.
Tel: 0171 607 3637 / Fax: 0171 607 3629
e-mail: oberon.books@btinternet.com

British Library Cataloguing-in-Publication Data
A catalogue record for this book is available from the British
Library.

ISBN 1 84002 033 4

Cover design: Andrzej Klimowski

Typography: Richard Doust

Printed in Great Britain by Arrowhead Books Ltd., Reading.

for Bill and Pearl

SUGAR SUGAR was first performed at the Bush Theatre, on 8th July 1998, with the following cast:

VAL, Sue Johnston

STEVEN, Nicolas Tennant

DENNIS WILSON, Jonny Phillips

LEA, Edward Peel

SHIRLEY, Deborah McAndrew

JOE, Andrew Lincoln

Directed by Paul Miller

Designed by Jess Curtiss

Lighting designed by Andy Phillips

Sound by Alistair Westell

Characters

VAL

STEVEN

DENNIS WILSON

LEN

SHIRLEY

JOE

Set in a guesthouse in Scarborough.

The present.

The action takes place in the breakfast room of the guest house. The room is half covered in dust sheets, the carpet up, tins of half empty and full paint, brushes and rollers. Lining paper on the walls, half painted. There are three tables, one is set proper and the other two are covered in tools and decorating materials. One exit leads to the kitchen and through to a back yard and entry. The other exit leads to the hall, front door, and rest of the house.

ACT ONE

Scene 1

STEVEN and VAL. Breakfast room.

STEVEN sat at a table eating.

Vases of flowers on all the tables but for the one STEVEN is eating at.

The sound of hammering offstage.

Enter VAL with a vase of flowers and puts it on the table that STEVEN is eating at.

She arranges the flowers. STEVEN moves his plate slightly to one side, out of her way.

STEVEN: Oh, sorry.

> *She finishes arranging the flowers and looks around the room.*

VAL: There.

STEVEN: Yeah, very – very.

VAL: I like a bit of colour.

STEVEN: Yeah, it's nice.

LEN: (*Offstage.*) Arrgh!

STEVEN: I've said I'd do it for him.

VAL: He likes to do it himself.

STEVEN: Yeah.

VAL: I had to wait five years for a washing line.

STEVEN: How's Shirley?

VAL: I've washed my hands.

STEVEN: She's lost her handbag.

VAL: It breaks my heart. Going off with a married man like that. There's no talking to her, she's gone mental. Nothing good will come of it, he goes home to his wife at the weekends and they've got a little kiddie. A daughter of mine. A home wrecker. She's breaking my heart. And when it's all done she'll be back, tail between her legs, crying on my shoulder. Well I won't have it, I'm not having it. She wants to live like that she's on her own.

STEVEN: I should stop coming round.

VAL: Don't be ridiculous – just because she wants to act like a fool doesn't mean you should have to go without your dinner.

STEVEN: It doesn't feel right.

VAL: And when it's all over, don't go out with her again.

STEVEN: No, I won't.

VAL: Let her pick herself up out the gutter.

STEVEN: Yeah.

VAL: If she can.

STEVEN: He's stopped banging.

Enter DENNIS. With mug.

VAL: Oh Mister Wilson, you're up early – we don't normally see you till well after the sun's gone down.

DENNIS: He's fixing the floorboards.

STEVEN: Been out stretching your wings, have you?

DENNIS: (*Holding out mug.*) It's just – I just –

VAL: Oh, give it here.

She takes the mug.

DENNIS: I need some hot water.

VAL: Honestly, men.

She goes to exit.

DENNIS: I'll get it myself.

VAL: I'll get it.

DENNIS: Are you sure.

VAL: Why not, I do it for everyone else.

Exit VAL into kitchen.

STEVEN: Now then. How's it going?

DENNIS: Alright. You.

STEVEN: Can't complain. How's the gardening?

DENNIS: Slow.

STEVEN: Aye – gets like that round here in winter.

DENNIS: I like it.

STEVEN: You should try working on the boats.

DENNIS: Have you worked on the boats?

STEVEN: No – but a mate I've got has, in the galley. Can you cook?

DENNIS: No.

STEVEN: I can't cook. (*Loud.*) Auntie Val can cook, she's a great cook. Anything you can fit in a frying pan – I don't fancy it, all those blokes at sea in a boat.

STEVEN pushes his plate away.

Enter VAL with DENNIS's mug.

STEVEN burps.

Sorry about that auntie Val.

VAL: Would you like milk with it Mister Wilson?

DENNIS: No thanks.

STEVEN: If I were an Arab, that would've been a compliment.

VAL: I could heat some cottage pie up for you, if you like.

STEVEN: What sort of tea do you call that?

DENNIS: It's herbal.

STEVEN: Oh, I see.

DENNIS: Are you his auntie?

VAL: No.

DENNIS: Thanks for the water.

VAL: I'll save you some cottage pie.

DENNIS: Thanks.

> *Exit DENNIS.*

STEVEN: What's wrong with tea.

VAL: Nothing.

STEVEN: Exactly. Dracula.

VAL: Steven.

STEVEN: Right. (*He stands.*) I have to go, I'm on at six
    thirty – double shift. I'll see thee later then auntie Val.
    Don't I get a kiss goodbye then auntie Val.

VAL: No.

STEVEN: Why not, auntie Val.

VAL: Because you don't deserve one.

STEVEN: I ate all my dinner. Give us a kiss auntie Val,
    please auntie Val.

VAL: Steven, behave.

STEVEN: Go on, give us a kiss, kiss us, kiss me auntie Val.

He chases after her round the tables.

Just one little kiss auntie Val –

Enter LEN with electric hand-drill.

STEVEN stops chasing VAL.

STEVEN and VAL laugh.

STEVEN goes to leave and passes LEN.

STEVEN: Len.

LEN: Bloody hammer.

Exit STEVEN.

Anything happen on the news?

VAL: They've extended voting in central Africa somewhere because it's going so well, police in Gloucestershire are on the lookout for a sex fiend with a limp and half the electricity in this country is now owned by Americans.

LEN: It's a bloody disgrace.

VAL: You want a cup of tea.

LEN: No thanks.

VAL: You want a cup of tea.

LEN: No I don't.

VAL: You're sure you don't want a cup of tea.

LEN: I'll have coffee later.

He sits and puts drill on table.

VAL: What have you been doing?

LEN: What do you think I've been doing.

VAL: How do I know, you know what you've been doing, how do I know.

The phone rings.

VAL picks up the phone.

LEN reads his paper.

Hello, the Seatos guesthouse. Who are you? Are you the hospital? Is it serious? Are you his family? I'm afraid I'm not at liberty to give out the names of our guests to unknown strangers. It's the law. I never said that. If there is a Mister Wilson staying with us I will tell him you called. Goodbye.

She puts the phone down.

LEN: A man in Liverpool has accidentally killed his daughter. He fixed a fuse with ordinary wire, she takes a shower, there's an electrical fault, the fuse doesn't blow and she's electrocuted naked in the shower.

VAL: Poor man.

LEN: He claims it was an accident.

VAL: Why would he kill his own daughter?

LEN: Maybe he didn't like her.

VAL: I've never liked showers.

LEN: Me neither.

VAL: You don't like water.

LEN: I love swimming.

VAL: You're shrinking.

LEN: Just make the coffee.

VAL: You are you're shrinking.

LEN: I'll shrink if I want, now make the coffee.

VAL: Make it yourself.

LEN: Flowers – what have we got flowers for – you might as well throw good money down the drain.

VAL: I like flowers, it's November.

LEN: So what, what's wrong with November, I like November.

VAL: You've got no heart.

LEN: There's nothing wrong with my heart – I'm not dying yet, not by a long chalk, you don't get rid of me that easy.

VAL: You've got no feelings.

LEN: It's you – you haven't got a good word to say about anyone or anything, you never bloody have had.

VAL: Please don't swear.

LEN: All these years I've had to put up with you going on.

VAL: It's my nerves.

LEN: You've got tablets haven't you – what do you want to take tablets for anyway?

VAL: I'm all feelings.

LEN: I get miserable, we all get miserable, but I don't take tablets – I get up, I go out, I do something, anything – I make myself useful – I don't wallow in misery stuck indoors – you've been stewing in the stuff for years, you don't know anything else but feeling sorry for yourself.

VAL: You've got no heart.

LEN: Fit heart, fit lungs, I could run a marathon.

VAL: What about your legs?

LEN: Never a good word to say about anything.

Silence.

VAL: Another little boy's gone missing. His mother was on the news...

She is near to tears.

People are wicked... the world is wicked... and she – she could hardly speak for tears... she'd lost her little boy...

LEN: It's taken hundreds of years to get where we are now – and it's getting worse – three hundred years ago they chopped off your hand for stealing, hung you and sent you to Australia.

VAL: What do you want for tea?

LEN: Chop off people's hands and you'd soon put a stop to all this child molesting.

VAL: What do you want to eat?

Enter SHIRLEY.

Steven's been looking for you.

SHIRLEY: Well I don't want to see him.

LEN: You treat that boy like dirt.

SHIRLEY: I treat him the way he lets himself be treated.

LEN: Oh, so you'd rather he hit you.

SHIRLEY: No.

VAL: What's he done wrong then – wrong enough that you have to go off with a married man.

SHIRLEY: Nothing, he's done nothing, right. Why does my life have to be so bloody public –

LEN: Don't swear at your mother.

SHIRLEY: It's private alright, it's between Steven and me.

VAL: He's still coming round for his dinner.

SHIRLEY: So?

VAL: I'm just saying.

SHIRLEY: I don't care, it doesn't bother me, he can do what he likes – he can jump off Valley Bridge with no clothes on and kill himself for all I care.

VAL: You've changed.

SHIRLEY buries her head in her hands and screams.

Why do you have to upset everyone.

SHIRLEY: It's you, you, you –

VAL: And everyone always used to say what a lovely little girl you were. And now look at you. A tramp.

LEN: Pack it in.

VAL: You've lost your handbag.

SHIRLEY: How did you know?

VAL: I know.

SHIRLEY: How do you know?

VAL: I know everything.

LEN: Pack it in.

VAL: What have I done, I'm not doing anything.

SHIRLEY makes a move towards VAL.

Go on then, I dare you.

LEN: You keep your hands off your mother.

SHIRLEY: (*To VAL.*) I hate you.

LEN: Stop it, you hear me, just stop it.

SHIRLEY: I wish you were dead.

VAL: You shouldn't say that, you'll regret saying that.

SHIRLEY: I do, I wish you were dead.

Exit SHIRLEY.

VAL: (*Shouts after her.*) I'll die in the night and you'll wish you never said that. My own family. My own family. It's a mess.

LEN: I'll have cottage pie.

VAL: No you won't.

LEN: I want cottage pie.

VAL: Well you can't have it, I've promised it Mister Wilson. I'll do you some beans.

LEN: I don't want beans. What d'you promise my cottage pie to him for?

VAL: It's not your cottage pie.

LEN: Well whose is it then?

VAL: He's a guest. He pays his lodgings.

LEN: No he doesn't, he claims for it all back in benefits – we're paying, that's who's paying, we're paying for him to stay in our own bloody house.

VAL: I like to make all our guests feel welcome.

LEN: Did Steven have cottage pie?

VAL: Yes.

LEN: Right, that's it, I'm having chips.

VAL: Do you think Mister Wilson will like the flowers?

LEN: You're making a fool of yourself. You're old enough to be his mother, and Steven's.

VAL: Have you finished your banging, in the hall.

LEN: You just watch it, I've got my eye on you.

LEN picks up drill.

VAL: So, you're going to drill something now are you.

LEN: Your head if you don't watch it. A leopard doesn't change its spots.

VAL: Any fool can make himself busy.

Enter DENNIS.

LEN: You should know, you've had years of experience. What do you think of the flowers son?

DENNIS: Yeah, I like them.

LEN: Bloody funeral parlour.

Exit LEN.

DENNIS: I'll come back later. Are you alright, is everything alright?

VAL: Yes, yes. Thankyou. Sometimes I think I could give it all up and just run away.

DENNIS: What would you do?

VAL: Nothing. I'd sit on a beach all day and do nothing. I'd find somewhere nice and die quietly. I don't want to die but sometimes I wish I was dead. You don't have children.

DENNIS: No.

VAL: You don't sound very certain.

DENNIS: No I'm not.

VAL: You had a wild youth.

DENNIS: No.

VAL: I'll get you your cottage pie.

DENNIS: No, thankyou – I'm not hungry – I just need some more water.

VAL: I've got some cheese.

DENNIS: Just some water please.

VAL: Hot or cold?

DENNIS: Cold.

VAL: (*Takes his mug.*) I'll get you a glass.

DENNIS: Thankyou.

> *Exit VAL into kitchen.*
>
> *He sits at table and pulls petals off a flower.*
>
> *Enter VAL with glass of water.*
>
> *DENNIS takes the glass off her.*

DENNIS: Thankyou.

They were dying.

VAL: You've had a phone call Mister Wilson.

DENNIS: Oh.

VAL: Yes.

DENNIS: Who was it?

VAL: I don't know, they wouldn't say. They asked to speak to Mister Wilson and I asked who they were and they wouldn't say, all they said was that it was personal – I asked if it was the hospital, but they said no. There's nothing wrong is there?

DENNIS: No.

VAL: You're not expecting a call?

DENNIS: No.

VAL: It was a man.

DENNIS: Thanks, thankyou for telling me.

VAL: I expect they'll ring back.

DENNIS: Yeah. Beautiful flowers.

VAL: Oh, I'm glad you like them. I suppose you have to like flowers in your line of business, imagine a gardener that didn't like flowers.

DENNIS: I don't like gardens.

VAL: I had you down for a man of taste the moment I met you, you reminded me of that man in the advert for hair spray.

You were in Scotland.

DENNIS: Yes.

VAL: But you're not Scottish.

DENNIS: No.

She laughs.

VAL: That's nice. You're all settled in. You didn't bring much with you, did you?

DENNIS: I had to – I was in a rush, when I left.

VAL: Oh.

DENNIS: Nothing serious.

VAL: A spot of bother. At home.

DENNIS: Yeah.

VAL: A girlfriend.

DENNIS: Yeah, yeah.

VAL: So, you've left your heart in Scotland.

DENNIS drinks glass of water.

Don't mind me I'm just naturally inquisitive. We went to the west coast once, the Outer Hebrides. It was glorious, do you know them?

DENNIS: No, no – but I hear that they are.

VAL: Oh yes, we went in a camper van – it was glorious.

DENNIS: You're not the first person to tell me.

VAL: Are you thirsty?

DENNIS: Yes.

VAL: Would you like some proper tea?

DENNIS: No thanks.

VAL: Go on, I'll put the kettle on.

DENNIS: Alright.

VAL: It's Yorkshire tea.

DENNIS: Nice.

VAL: How would you like it.

DENNIS: Oh – milk, no sugar. Do you mind if I smoke?

VAL: No, no, not at all.

He takes out a tobacco tin and a small ornate box, like a snuff box. He puts them on the table and opens the tobacco tin.

I'll put the kettle on.

Exit VAL.

DENNIS rolls a cigarette.

Enter VAL with ashtray.

It's from Madeira.

She watches him finish rolling cigarette.

What's the little one for?

DENNIS: Oh, you know, this and that.

DENNIS lights up.

VAL: My father's father rolled his own cigarettes, in the trenches.

DENNIS: Your grandfather.

VAL: That's right. I never knew him of course. He got knocked down by a tram on his way back from the pub, him and Willy Burgess, he was riding cross bar on Willy's bike. Do you like to drink?

DENNIS: Now and again, you know.

VAL: He liked to drink.

DENNIS: I like my room.

VAL: It was the death of him.

DENNIS: Yeah.

VAL: Yes – the both of them.

She laughs.

DENNIS: The room suits me.

VAL: Are you sure you wouldn't like some cottage pie?

DENNIS: Maybe later.

VAL: I like to drink in the Black Lion, we call it the Dead Cat – hardly anyone goes in there but it's clean – I don't suppose you know it? I'll have to take you up there one night, we'll have a drink. (*Pause.*) Yes. You should take up modelling – you look like one of the men out of my catalogue.

DENNIS stubs out cigarette.

DENNIS: Thanks for the water.

VAL: What about your tea?

DENNIS: Later – thanks, thankyou, thanks – I'll see you later.

Exit DENNIS.

VAL picks up his cigarette and sniffs it. She lights it cautiously and takes several quick sharp drags, as though it might blow up. She coughs and stubs it out.

Exit VAL.

Scene 2

STEVEN and JOE.

Enter STEVEN and JOE. STEVEN carrying JOE's bag.

STEVEN: I don't know why you want to live down there – we've got everything you've got down there up here, only it's closer together. I wouldn't fancy living down there.

STEVEN puts JOE's bag on a table.

JOE: Not on the table.

STEVEN: Right.

STEVEN puts bag on floor.

You fancy a spliff?

JOE: No thanks.

STEVEN: I fancy a spliff. We're not supposed to while driving. You have a spliff.

JOE: I don't want to.

STEVEN: Go on, do you good.

JOE: I'm alright.

STEVEN: Have a spliff.

JOE: She won't like it.

STEVEN: She won't mind.

JOE: She will.

STEVEN: She won't I'm telling you, she likes me your mam.

JOE: Well I mind.

STEVEN: Don't be soft, you're on holiday.

JOE: No I'm not.

STEVEN: So what you come home for then?

JOE: Nothing, right.

STEVEN: Alright.

Gives cash to STEVEN.

STEVEN: No, I can't.

JOE: Go on.

STEVEN: It's alright.

JOE: You've earnt it.

STEVEN: I don't want your money.

JOE: You must be doing alright.

STEVEN: Yeah, not so bad.

JOE: Mini cabbing suits you.

STEVEN: I'm just doing it till something better comes
    along – alright.

JOE: Alright.

STEVEN: It's like you just popped round the corner for a packet of fags.

JOE: What about you and my sister.

STEVEN: What about us?

JOE: She give you the boot.

STEVEN: No she never.

JOE: That's not what I heard.

STEVEN: Well you heard wrong then.

JOE: Flowers, she does it every year, fills the house with flowers.

STEVEN: I like your trousers.

JOE: Moleskin.

STEVEN: Smart. Here, Rosemary Tredwell works in our office.

JOE: She never.

STEVEN: She does – on the phones. She came up the drivers room this morning and I thought, "Let's have a fuck, in the toilet."

JOE: You should've said.

STEVEN: I know.

JOE: She would.

STEVEN: I know.

JOE: You should have.

STEVEN: I will. Tomorrow's her last day, she's getting married.

Enter SHIRLEY.

SHIRLEY: What are you doing here?

JOE: It's my home.

SHIRLEY: What's he doing here?

JOE: Don't I get a kiss or anything?

SHIRLEY: No, you haven't been gone away long enough. And as for you Steven Best you can stop sniffing round our house, there's nothing here for you.

STEVEN: I'm not sniffing, he's my fare.

SHIRLEY: Go home with all your fares do you?

STEVEN: That's not right, you know that's not right, I never.

SHIRLEY: Oh yeah?

STEVEN: Yeah – not even the once.

JOE: Where's mam?

SHIRLEY: Yeah, right.

STEVEN: What do you think I am, stupid?

JOE: Where's mam?

SHIRLEY: Out.

STEVEN: It's more than my job's worth.

SHIRLEY gets out lipstick and does her lips.

This one lad right, he did it with this girl on his back seat and it turns out she's under sixteen and now she's having him for rape, he's lost everything, his job, his home, everything. It's hard to tell what's what nowadays.

JOE: You look nice. Where are you going?

SHIRLEY: Nowhere.

STEVEN: The Underground, that's where she works.

SHIRLEY: Shut up Steven.

JOE: In a night club. But it's early yet.

SHIRLEY: I'm responsible for the bar.

STEVEN: We've got the contract for taking the staff home.

SHIRLEY: Belt up Steven.

JOE: You do, you look smashing.

STEVEN: She's off out to break someone's heart.

JOE: What's that lipstick?

SHIRLEY: Strawberry flavour.

STEVEN: Femme fatale flavour. Has it been tested on animals?

SHIRLEY: No, not yet.

STEVEN: Go on, give us a kiss.

SHIRLEY: Get lost.

STEVEN: If I had the money, I'd just pack my bags now and get on a plane to Spain.

JOE: Yeah, Spain, rent a villa in Spain.

STEVEN: We could all go.

JOE: Yeah.

STEVEN: We'd let Shirley come 'n all, if she promised to behave.

JOE: She could do the cooking.

SHIRLEY: I'm not going to Spain.

STEVEN: No, come on, come to Spain with us.

JOE: Yeah, Spain.

SHIRLEY: I don't want to go to Spain.

STEVEN: No, no, we'd have fun.

SHIRLEY: You go to Spain, you two go to Spain, I'm not going to Spain, I wouldn't be seen dead in Spain.

Exit SHIRLEY.

STEVEN: You want a joint? I want a joint.

JOE: You can't, you're driving.

STEVEN: You sure you don't want a joint?

JOE: Yes.

STEVEN: Alright, we won't have a joint. You're sure?

JOE: Steven.

STEVEN: I'll have a joint, I'll skin up a joint.

STEVEN starts to roll a joint.

JOE: Come on, I'll buy you a drink.

STEVEN continues to roll joint.

STEVEN: I don't know why you want to live down there. What have you got down there, that we haven't got up here?

JOE: Nothing.

STEVEN: We've got everything.

JOE: Yeah.

STEVEN: Yeah.

JOE: Come on, let's go for a drink.

STEVEN: I can't, I'm working.

JOE: What about that?

STEVEN: What.

JOE: Take the afternoon off.

STEVEN: What for?

JOE: I'll buy you a drink.

STEVEN: Alright.

JOE: We'll go up the Star.

STEVEN: You won't like it.

JOE: I like drinking in the Star.

STEVEN: I'm not drinking in the Star.

JOE: We're going up the Star.

STEVEN: Alright.

> *Exit JOE and STEVEN.*

Scene 3

LEN sat gazing blankly up at the wall facing the audience.

SHIRLEY writing at a table at the back.

Enter VAL with dirty sheets.

VAL: I've made up his bed.

> *Exit VAL into the kitchen.*
>
> *Silence.*
>
> *Enter VAL.*

VAL: You haven't got the sound up.

LEN: It's broke.

VAL: Get it fixed then.

LEN: It'll do as it is.

VAL: It'll do, it'll do, if I hear it'll do one more time in this house I'll go mad.

Exit VAL into kitchen.

LEN: (*Shouts off.*) I like looking at the pictures.

SHIRLEY: Shut up will you.

Enter VAL.

She sits and watches with LEN.

VAL: Who are you writing to?

SHIRLEY: Nobody.

LEN: I'm hot. I bet you're cold.

VAL: She's writing to him.

LEN: You're not cold.

VAL: No. To the adulterer.

SHIRLEY: What's it to you?

VAL: Nothing. Throw your life away, see if I care.

LEN: What are you then?

VAL: I'm not hot and I'm not cold.

LEN: So, you're alright.

VAL: I didn't say that.

LEN: Well, what are you then? You're either hot or cold, you've got to be one or the other – you can't not be.

VAL: There's a slight chill in the air.

LEN: You're cold.

VAL: No I'm not.

LEN: Yes you are – you said, she just said, I heard you with my own ears. You heard, go on, tell her, tell her you heard.

SHIRLEY: What do I care?

LEN: She's your mother.

VAL: She's writing to him, her adulterous lover. Animals.

Silence.

VAL shudders.

All those ice cream vans in the countryside. They spoil it. They're unhygienic. Selling beefburgers in unhygienic baps.

SHIRLEY: I hate the countryside.

JOE: (*Offstage.*) I burnt her coat.

VAL: You don't like anything beautiful.

Enter JOE and STEVEN from the kitchen.

JOE props up STEVEN.

JOE: Hello mam, I'm back.

VAL: So I see.

JOE: He's alright.

STEVEN: I'm alright, there's nowt wrong with me.

STEVEN sits at table opposite SHIRLEY.

VAL: How's your wife?

JOE: The wife's alright, my wife is alright.

STEVEN: I love you guys, I do, I do, I really do.

LEN slips off his shoes.

JOE: I burnt her coat – she can't be trusted, she's a liar, she's a woman.

STEVEN: So, you're writing a letter then.

LEN: It's a curse having sweaty feet.

Exit SHIRLEY upstairs.

Exit VAL into kitchen.

What – what – where are you going? That's the thanks I get is it – they're clean, my feet are clean –

Enter VAL with air freshener and sprays room.

I wash them every night in consideration of others – well I won't bother now, from now on I'll let them smell, it doesn't bother me, I don't mind, it's no skin off my nose.

JOE: She's the most poisonous, stupid, selfish, cruel, thoughtless... I've ever had the misfortune to... Worthless, nothing, sentimental – the only thing that can upset her, really upset her, is the death of a dog, a cat, an animal, a pet – There's nothing more to her than – you couldn't drown in her – grab, grab, grab, grab all she can, no matter what – for love, to be loved...

VAL: She's found herself another man again.

JOE: I'm not going back, I'm never going back.

VAL: I told you not to marry her.

JOE: I want all my cutlery and the television set back. I came home and they'd gone, she'd gone – but I didn't know, I didn't think, you don't know – they were gone, her and the baby, my baby, she's taken my baby, she took my baby, my child – she's taken my child – I didn't know, I didn't think you don't know – she rang at seven thirty the next morning, I got out of bed and I said, "It's seven thirty in the morning and I'm naked."

33

VAL: What did she say?

JOE: She asked if I was cold.

STEVEN: And were you?

JOE: She's taken my baby, she took my baby.

JOE drops his head in his hands.

VAL: I've made your bed up.

Enter SHIRLEY.

STEVEN: There are some people I'd very much like to talk to naked on the phone.

SHIRLEY: Well go and do it then.

STEVEN: They don't know me and I haven't got their numbers.

He reaches across the table and strokes her hand.

Are you writing to him on perfumed paper?

She pulls her hand away.

SHIRLEY: You live in a dream world.

JOE: I hate women – no, no, I don't mean that – yes, yes I do – it was only a joke. Twice this week, twice I've had to tell her to shut up – and when I say shut up I mean shut up.

VAL: It's the child I feel sorry for.

STEVEN: If I want to live in a dream world then I bloody well will – Ooohps, sorry auntie Val.

VAL: That child doesn't stand a chance.

JOE: That child, that child – she's my daughter, she's got a name, you use my daughter's name, I love my daughter.

Exit JOE into the kitchen.

STEVEN: Here, you'll never guess what.

SHIRLEY: What?

Exit VAL into the kitchen.

STEVEN: We just saw this bloke right, walking down the street, two wooden legs – two wooden legs and real feet.

LEN stands up and goes to exit.

LEN: And nobody touch that television set.

Exit LEN.

STEVEN: Two wooden legs and real feet.

SHIRLEY: Yeah?

STEVEN: Yeah.

SHIRLEY: Fuck off.

STEVEN: Now what – what have I done?

SHIRLEY: Nothing.

STEVEN: What did I do?

SHIRLEY: Nothing.

STEVEN: No, come on, come on – out with it.

SHIRLEY: Nothing, there's nothing to say.

STEVEN: Ah, don't get like that.

She writes and STEVEN watches her.

JOE: (*Offstage.*) I can't – I won't – I can't, I'll never – you hear me, never – it was her, all her.

STEVEN: I'm different now Shirley.

SHIRLEY: Oh yeah?

STEVEN: I am – honest, I am – I've changed, I'm different, I'm not the same person anymore. It wouldn't be the same anymore. I've learned to cry, I have – I've cried in front of my best mate.

SHIRLEY: Who's that then?

STEVEN: Whatsit – you know, whatshisface – I have Shirley, he was this close and I cried, I wept buckets.

SHIRLEY moves away.

What, what?

SHIRLEY: You're breathing beer in my face.

STEVEN: I tell you, since we stopped – since you stopped – since we stopped going out and I haven't had any phone calls – you ringing up telling me what a bastard I am – I've had a laugh, I mean me and Joe have had a laugh about it, a real laugh, no more phone calls telling me what a bastard I am.

SHIRLEY: So what are you doing here then?

STEVEN: There are three reasons why people get married, right. Right. One – because she gets knocked up – up the duff – two... because it's cheaper – money, mortgages – and three.... three...

SHIRLEY: Because they love each other.

STEVEN: Yeah, yeah – and three because her parents don't like him and it makes him want to marry her all the more. Well fuck that, I went out with you because I wanted you – because I thought if I don't go out with Shirley somebody else will. I wanted you.

SHIRLEY: Steven.

STEVEN: What?

SHIRLEY: You're ugly.

STEVEN: I love you.

SHIRLEY: Oh, grow up.

Enter LEN.

He sits and watches the telly.

STEVEN: You can't move on unless you're happy where you are.

Enter VAL.

VAL: Steven, go home and get into bed.

STEVEN: I love you auntie Val, I love you.

LEN: Millions of years ago – before man had been born – there were all sorts of strange creatures floating about, swimming around in the sea – giant brains – nothing else, just a brain in the ocean.

STEVEN: What did it think?

LEN: Nothing.

VAL: Steven – bed, now.

STEVEN: Hang on, hang on – how big is this brain?

LEN: As big as this house.

SHIRLEY: Where's Joe?

VAL: Washing his hair.

STEVEN: So, there's this giant brain right, as big as this house, floating around in the middle of the ocean, yeah?

LEN: Yeah.

STEVEN: So, what did it think?

LEN: About what?

STEVEN: Are you trying to be funny? It can't just have thought nothing, it had to think something, it was a brain.

SHIRLEY: Why not, you've got a brain and you don't think anything.

STEVEN: Oh, I see – I see – you're having me on.

LEN: I've seen the fossils to prove it.

SHIRLEY: Yeah.

LEN: Go home Steven, go on.

STEVEN: You've seen a fossilised brain.

Your fossil, his fossil dropped off years ago.

VAL: Steven.

STEVEN: Do you polish your fossil, is that what you do every night when you go to bed – polish your fossil.

SHIRLEY: Steven, grow up.

LEN: Go home son, come on.

LEN goes to help STEVEN.

STEVEN: It's alright, I'm alright – I can manage, I'm going. If you can't see it, if you can't smell it, if you can't touch it, then it doesn't exist.

Enter DENNIS carrying a book.

Night then, Dracula.

Exit STEVEN.

VAL: Oh, Mister Wilson – we're watching the television. You don't watch the television.

DENNIS: I watch the telly, I like the telly.

VAL: Len's got the sound down, he likes looking at the pictures.

They all watch television. SHIRLEY reads a travel magazine.

You've got a scar on your chin.

DENNIS: Yes.

VAL: When they first started this game show, because it's based on an American game show, as most of our game shows are, there were complaints. People complained that the prizes were too expensive.

DENNIS: I was just going to make a cup of tea.

VAL: Mind you, they're not bad now.

LEN: Shut up will you.

Silence.

VAL: You remind me of my brother Paul. What do you think Len?

LEN: What?

VAL: Mister Wilson reminds me of our Paul.

LEN: He looks nothing like Paul.

VAL: And that man in the advert.

LEN: What advert?

VAL: For hair spray. You do, you remind me of our Paul.

Enter JOE. Wet hair and naked to the waist with a towel hanging round his neck. He rubs his hair dry with the towel.

LEN turns off the telly.

LEN: What's all the racket for, why all the racket – I'm trying to watch the telly.

Exit LEN.

VAL: Joe, this is Mister Wilson, Mister Wilson this is my son Joe.

JOE: Now then.

DENNIS: Pleased to meet you.

VAL: Joe – Joe's come home for a few days.

JOE: Wilson, your name's Wilson.

DENNIS: Yes.

JOE: Mister Wilson. Have you got any other names?

DENNIS: Yes, Dennis.

JOE: Dennis.

VAL: Dennis.

SHIRLEY: Dennis.

VAL looks at SHIRLEY.

I've never met anyone called Dennis before.

JOE: So, what do you do for a living Dennis?

DENNIS: I'm a gardener.

JOE: And when you're not gardening?

DENNIS: Nothing.

JOE: I see.

DENNIS: I'm a seasonal worker.

JOE: Right.

DENNIS: Sometimes I work.

JOE: Really.

DENNIS: Yes.

VAL: Mister Wilson was in Scotland before he came here. He's left his heart in Scotland.

DENNIS: Yeah.

JOE: So, what are you doing here then?

DENNIS: Nothing much.

JOE: Nothing much what?

DENNIS: This and that, you know.

JOE: How did you get here?

DENNIS: On the coach.

JOE: Where are you going?

DENNIS: I don't know.

JOE: Where would you like to go?

DENNIS: Nottingham.

JOE: Why Nottingham?

DENNIS: I've never been.

SHIRLEY: He had a girlfriend lived in Nottingham.

JOE: I'm not talking to you, am I?

SHIRLEY: Alright, no need to get shirty.

JOE: I'm not.

DENNIS: What do you do Joe?

JOE: I live here. Night then, mam.

JOE kisses VAL and exits.

VAL: It's best not to ask. You should get yourself another girlfriend Mister Wilson.

DENNIS: No, I don't think so – I've given all that up.

VAL: Yes. A handsome young man like you wouldn't have any trouble taking his pick of the bunch.

DENNIS: Oh yeah – I get chased after by young girls all the time.

VAL: He doesn't like people asking. He goes to work early and doesn't get back till late the next morning. He has to spend night after night in hotel rooms all over the country, and at least once in Holland that I know of.

SHIRLEY: My boyfriend lived in Holland for eight years.

DENNIS: Oh, what did he do?

VAL: We don't want to know.

SHIRLEY: He worked in a salad cream factory. Then he met a local girl, got married, had two kids and moved to Paris.

VAL: I shouldn't really say this –

SHIRLEY: They live in Bridlington now.

VAL: You'll promise you won't say. My son is an undercover accountant. He follows accountants, all over the world sometimes. I don't really understand it. He's not at liberty to talk about his work in public. He's signed confidentiality agreements and sworn oaths of secrecy. Sometimes he gets followed and has to go into hiding. He drives an old battered Ford white van so as not to arouse suspicion. We think he's been to New York. I shouldn't be saying any of this. He doesn't like drawing attention to himself. You won't let him know I've told you.

DENNIS: No, I won't.

VAL: He's working on a big case at the moment. That's why he gets so fraught. That and his wife.

SHIRLEY: They're not married.

VAL: They've got a child. Where are you going?

SHIRLEY: I like looking at the pictures.

VAL: It's got something to do with the Mafia and he has to talk about it in code. There, I've said too much already – I've got such a big mouth, but I thought it best you know. We're in no real danger though. He won't say much more about it, the less we know the better.

DENNIS: Yes.

SHIRLEY: The whole street knows.

VAL: We can't say anything then can we.

DENNIS: No, I see.

VAL: No one can make us say anything he doesn't want them to know, not even accidentally.

DENNIS: Right.

VAL: And if any of his friends come round, don't say anything about his work – they might not be who they appear to be.

SHIRLEY: What about Steven?

VAL: What about him?

SHIRLEY: How do you know he's who he says he is.

VAL: Oh, don't be ridiculous.

Enter LEN and picks up a paint brush and pot of paint.

LEN: I've got no time for people who are good to you when you're dead or dying – what's the good in that – it's easy to be nice to you when you're dead, it's easy to smile and be good to the dead.

LEN looks at SHIRLEY.

She's a waste of time – a bloody costume on a coat hanger, she's got no dignity, with this man and that. Good night then.

VAL *and* DENNIS *and* SHIRLEY: Night.

VAL: Have you much family Mister Wilson?

DENNIS: Dennis.

VAL: Dennis.

SHIRLEY: Dennis.

VAL looks at SHIRLEY.

Well it's true, you're the first Dennis I've ever met.

VAL: What about your family Dennis?

SHIRLEY: I've got a shirt like that.

VAL: Is it very big.

SHIRLEY: Exactly the same colour.

VAL: Is it big Mister Wilson?

DENNIS: Yes.

SHIRLEY: What size chest have you got?

DENNIS: No, no – I haven't got a very big family.

SHIRLEY: Dennis the Menace.

VAL: Shirley.

SHIRLEY: What? I'm only joking, Mister Wilson knows how to take a joke, don't you Dennis.

DENNIS: Yeah.

VAL: You do, you look just like man off the advert for hair spray, doesn't he Shirley? He looks just like that man in the advert for hair spray.

SHIRLEY: Yeah.

DENNIS: We've both got long hair.

VAL: No – you look like him.

Exit VAL.

SHIRLEY: You call that long?

DENNIS: It is for me. I did have it very long once.

SHIRLEY: I like long hair. You're reading a book. I like books. What's it about?

DENNIS: Myths.

SHIRLEY: We did them at school, which one are you reading?

DENNIS: The story of Atalanta.

SHIRLEY: What did she do?

DENNIS: She had a curse put on her, by Aphrodite.

SHIRLEY: Aphrodite.

DENNIS: Yeah. The Goddess of love.

SHIRLEY: The Goddess of love.

DENNIS: She could run so fast that no man could ever catch her.

SHIRLEY: That sounds like me. Are you alright? What's the matter?

DENNIS: Nothing.

SHIRLEY: We're going to enjoy having you here.

DENNIS: Right.

SHIRLEY: Yeah.

She feels his hair.

DENNIS pulls away slightly.

I'm only feeling your hair. It's dry. Can I have a look at your book?

He gives her the book.

She opens the book.

You've written in it. "A star is a raging ball of fire and gas." What did you write that for?

DENNIS: I like the sound of it.

She gives him the book back. As she does so she strokes along the back of his hand.

SHIRLEY: Every September the universe expands.

Do you like mysteries?

DENNIS: Yes.

SHIRLEY: Yeah, so do I.

She goes to exit.

I read it on a pencil.

DENNIS: What?

SHIRLEY: About the universe.

Exit SHIRLEY.

Scene 4

VAL sat in the dark peeling potatoes.

Enter LEN.

LEN turns on the light.

LEN is wearing a dirty old orange cycle cape with the hood up, woolly hat, gloves and cycle clips.

LEN: It's snowing.

Exit LEN.

(*Offstage.*) Can I have a cup of tea?

VAL: Yes.

Enter LEN without cape gloves and hat.

LEN: Make me a cup of tea.

VAL: No.

LEN: (*Sings.*) "Fly me to the moon and I will dance among the stars, Jupiter and Venus – Pluto and Mars."

VAL: That's not how it goes.

LEN: You bleat.

VAL: It's not me that bleats, it's you that bleats. Make your own cup of tea.

LEN: I'm not making any tea.

VAL: I might as well be dead.

LEN: You think like a woman.

VAL: I am a woman.

LEN: I don't like your make-up, I don't like the lipstick you wear, I don't like your clothes and you don't speak properly.

VAL: I might as well be dead.

LEN: Go on then, do us all a favour, drop dead and stop your moaning woman.

VAL: Why did you never get married?

LEN: I had to look after you.

VAL: I can look after myself.

LEN: Oh, aye? He left you he walked out, the first sign of trouble and he was out that door – I've had to stay – three children and not all by the same father.

VAL picks up a vase of flowers and throws it at him.

VAL: You're cruel, selfish and stupid.

LEN: Go on then, go on – stab me.

She sits and peels potatoes.

VAL: I might as well be dead.

LEN: I'm not picking up the pieces.

The phone rings.

They look at each other and then the phone and then back at each other.

They hold the look.

VAL breaks the look and answers the phone.

VAL: Hello. She doesn't live here anymore.

VAL slams the phone down.

A married man and he's rung three times for her today. He's got no shame.

Wouldn't you like it better in the dining room?

LEN: No, I'm alright here.

VAL: You're sure you wouldn't be happier in the dining room.

LEN: No, I'm happy where I am.

VAL: Right.

She peels potatoes.

I think you'd be happier in the dining room.

LEN: No I wouldn't, honest.

VAL: It would be better for you in the dining room.

LEN: Do you want me to go in the dining room?

VAL: No.

LEN: If you want me to go just say.

VAL: That's not what I said, I'm not saying that. I'll be coming and going a lot, I've got the tea to make – I've got to water the plants – I've got to think, I need to think.

LEN: I'll go in the dining room then – all you have to do is say.

VAL: You'll be happier in the dining room.

LEN: No I won't.

VAL: You never do anything do you, you can't be relied on for anything.

LEN: I'm doing up the house.

VAL: And when's it going to be finished?

LEN: When it's finished, alright.

VAL: Right. I want the dining room done as well. Steven says he'll do it for us.

LEN: My arse.

VAL: I want the dining room done.

LEN: And let him make a pig's ear of it. Anything needs doing round here, I do it.

VAL: I want a chandelier.

LEN: What have we got a dining room for anyway? We never use it, when do we use it? Not even the guests use it, you just polish it, it's like a shrine.

VAL: It's for special occasions.

LEN: Yeah – birthdays, weddings and bloody funerals.

Exit VAL.

Now what – what have I done? (*Sings.*) "Fly me to the moon and I will show you all the stars – blah – blah – blah – blah – blah blah blah – blah blah blah blah blah blaaah – Jupiter and Mars."

Enter VAL.

VAL: That's not how it goes.

LEN: You bleat.

Exit LEN.

VAL turns off the light and sits in the dark.

Enter STEVEN from the kitchen.

STEVEN: (*Offstage.*) It's alright, it's only me auntie Val.

Comes into room carrying a handbag.

What you doing?

VAL: Oh, nothing.

STEVEN: I'll turn the light on then.

He turns on the light.

Peeling spuds.

VAL: Yes. I had an accident.

She picks up the flowers.

I'll put your tea on.

STEVEN: It's not tea yet, it's too early for tea.

VAL: Is it?

STEVEN: You've got your head screwed on back to front. I brought this round for Shirley, she left it in the back of one of our cars. I was just passing.

VAL: We used to get a lot of visitors.

STEVEN: People haven't got the money – it's the same with driving. She's not here then. I'll call back later.

VAL: No, don't go.

Silence.

STEVEN: Still not done. Is there anything you want?

VAL: No, it's alright, I'm alright.

STEVEN: Right, I'll be going then.

VAL: How old are you Steven?

STEVEN: What, me – twenty-nine. I don't think much of it me'self though – I'm looking forward to being forty-five, I'll be just about right by then, what do you think?

VAL: You shouldn't wish your life away, don't wish your life away Steven.

STEVEN: No, alright.

VAL: It's cold. I hate the winter.

STEVEN: What about Christmas?

VAL: The only thing I like about winter is going down to the front and watching the sea when it gets rough – everything else is dead or dying – I like watching the waves crash up against the sea wall, coming down like a thunderstorm on the road – we used to stand on those railings for hours waiting for a big one, a really big wave – and then we'd run, I'd really run – and I never got caught, I never got caught once by the sea – Johnny Pacito got dragged in one time and we had to call out the life boat.

STEVEN: What, him that's got the chip shop on the front.

VAL: Aye. I could have married him.

STEVEN: The fat bloke with no hair.

VAL: I hate the winter.

STEVEN: What about Christmas?

VAL: We're not having Christmas.

STEVEN: You can't not have Christmas.

VAL: We're not having Christmas, New Year neither. Are you coming back for your tea?

STEVEN: What are we having?

VAL: Gruel.

STEVEN: Yum, yum, auntie Val's gruel. Oh, you're bad to me auntie Val, I love you auntie Val.

He kisses her on the cheek.

VAL: Cheeky monkey.

STEVEN: I know.

Enter LEN.

LEN: Anything needs doing round here, I do it.

STEVEN: Alright uncle Len.

LEN: Don't you uncle me, I'm not your bloody uncle.

LEN turns on the television.

VAL: You can leave the bag with me, if you want.

STEVEN: No, no – it's alright.

Exit STEVEN.

VAL looks about her.

VAL: It's a mess – it's all a mess.

LEN: What's that then?

VAL: Turn that thing off.

LEN: I'm enjoying it.

VAL: Since when have you been interested in hot air ballooning?

LEN: You know what your trouble is don't you, you don't take enough interest in life – you want to broaden your horizons a bit, live a little.

VAL: Turn it off.

She turns it off.

LEN: I was enjoying that. You know what this is, it's discrimination – like against the disabled.

VAL: How do you want your potatoes?

LEN: And the blacks.

VAL: I don't know why you had to put that thing in here anyway.

LEN: It's not for me, it's for the visitors. It's capital expenditure. They like it with their breakfast.

VAL: They get enough of that at home – what do they want it here for as well? They come here to get away from it all.

LEN: I wish I could get away from it all.

VAL: Why don't you then?

LEN: Right away.

VAL: What's stopping you?

LEN: I will – one day I'll pack my bags and I'll be gone, and you'll be sorry then.

VAL: Oh, will I?

LEN: Yes, you will.

She picks up the potatoes.

VAL: Boiled or mash?

LEN: Both.

VAL: You can't have both.

LEN: Why not?

VAL: You'll get boiled.

LEN: So why ask?

VAL: To give you a choice.

Exit VAL.

LEN: Why can't I have both?

He turns on the television.

Enter VAL.

She turns off the television.

Choice – what choice have I got.

VAL: Boiled or mashed?

LEN: Nothing.

VAL: Fine, that's fine by me.

LEN: What do you care?

VAL: I don't.

LEN: Yeah.

VAL: Alright – you want boiled and mashed, have boiled and mashed – I'll make you boiled and mashed...

LEN: No thanks – I don't want anything.

VAL: You want boiled and mash.

LEN: No I don't.

VAL: Yes you do.

LEN: I don't.

VAL: Alright have nothing, see if I care.

Exit VAL.

LEN: If I want boiled and mashed potato I'll make it
myself, I don't need you to make it for me – I can look
after myself, I don't need you –

Enter JOE.

I don't need anyone.

JOE: Alright, no need to shout the houses down.

LEN: It's not me, it's her – you try doing something for her
and it's never good enough, it's always wrong – well it's
not me, it's her, it's her that's wrong.

JOE: What, what's wrong with her?

LEN: How should I know – her age, it's her bloody age –
she hasn't got the right hormones, she hasn't got enough
hormones. No wonder this country's in the mess it's in –
they put a woman in charge – she sent the Welsh guards
to their death and never cried, her son got lost in the
desert and she cried, the Welsh guards burned alive on the
Sir Galahad and she never cried. What I want is a long-
term relationship with a woman I don't have to live with.

Silence.

JOE: So, what's been going on in the world then dad?

LEN: How do I know, she won't even let me watch the telly.

JOE offers newspaper to LEN.

JOE: Have a read if you like.

LEN: You've got a paper?

JOE: The Evening News.

LEN: So why ask me what's going on in the world then?

JOE: Alright.

LEN: I've never understood women, I never will. I've kept a respectable distance from them all my life. As far as I can tell all they bring is trouble and it's not worth the bother. That's been my policy and it's done me no harm. You'd be well advised to do the same.

JOE: Says here the chancellor's sitting on a warchest, that there's going to be huge tax cuts just before the next general election.

LEN: There's too much tax all round.

JOE: They're just buying the electorate.

LEN: Who do you vote for?

JOE: It's plain as the nose on my face, even to a blind man.

LEN: The opposition always slates the government.

JOE: Who's the opposition?

LEN: You, you're the opposition.

Exit LEN.

JOE dials on his mobile phone.

JOE: It's Joe... He saw me. I couldn't help it. Yes, he's seen me before. I was walking past as he came out – so I went in and pretended to make enquiries – I was able to see him through the revolving doors – he got straight on his mobile... I'm not sure – his bodyguard –

Enter VAL.

He snaps phone shut.

The cow – the cow, I'll kill her.

VAL: Who's that?

JOE: Nobody.

VAL: Must be somebody.

JOE: It's nobody.

VAL: Alright, I don't want to know – I'm not getting involved – that's what you said, you don't want me poking my nose in your life. What I don't know can't hurt me. How do you think I feel – my daughter's a liar and a maniac – you don't believe me but she is – she attacked me naked in the bathroom with her boots on – and you, you – how you ever got involved with that woman I don't know.

Enter LEN with newspaper.

She whitewashed him so he couldn't think for himself. Where have you been?

LEN: To get the paper. Leave the lad alone.

VAL: He'd rather I say it to his face.

JOE: No I wouldn't. Why did she attack you?

VAL: She's a guttersnipe – breaking up a family like that, and there's a six year old kiddie involved – well I wish she'd leave, the sooner the better and have a breakdown.

JOE: You should keep your nose out.

LEN: Don't waste your breath son.

VAL: I thought you were packing your bags.

LEN: You'll be sorry when I'm gone, you'll see.

VAL: Why, what are you going to do, die. And what were you doing outside the St Nicholas hotel this dinner?

JOE: I wasn't.

VAL: I saw you.

JOE: It wasn't me.

VAL: You were lurking.

JOE: I was not lurking.

VAL: You were lurking, a grown man – behind the tide-table, opposite the revolving doors.

JOE: I was working.

VAL: You're not in any danger are you?

JOE: No mam.

LEN: I can't stop eating, I can't stop drinking, and I can't stop smoking.

VAL: You can't do anything.

JOE: I'm following Mister Big.

VAL: Mister Big.

LEN: Mister Big.

JOE: I can't tell you any more than that – other than if you breathe a word of this to anyone you'll put my life at risk. We none of us are in any immediate danger. He's responsible for the laundering of millions – pounds, dollars, marks, Swiss francs, the yen, all sorts, all over the world, by electronic transfer.

VAL: And he's in Scarborough?

JOE: He travels in disguise.

LEN: What sort of disguise?

JOE: I can't say any more.

VAL: You don't look well.

JOE: I feel fine.

LEN: I'd wear a wig, a pair of glasses and a false moustache.

VAL: You're not sleeping.

JOE: I'm sleeping.

VAL: You're not well.

JOE: I'm alright.

VAL: You don't look well.

JOE: I feel fine.

VAL: You're not yourself.

LEN: And a walking stick – maybe even a false limb.

VAL: You're not yourself.

JOE: Well if I'm not me who the bloody hell am I?

VAL: There's no need to swear at me, don't swear at me, I'm your mother – you can save your swearing for her – what have I done to deserve this?

JOE: You're my mother.

LEN: Then show her a bit of respect.

JOE: It's like being buried alive, the walking dead – this house, this house – it's like a grave.

VAL: What do you want with your stew?

JOE: I don't want any stew.

VAL: What do you want then?

JOE: I'm going out, out for a drink, alright.

VAL: You drink too much.

JOE: I like a drink.

VAL: You're killing yourself.

Enter DENNIS.

Oh, Mister Wilson, you've been out.

DENNIS: Yes – there was a meeting at the library I had to attend – the council wants to close the theatre to make way for twenty-two public toilets.

JOE: I have to go.

VAL: We're having stew.

LEN: That theatre's bled this town dry.

DENNIS: It's world-famous.

JOE: I'm going.

VAL: What about tea?

JOE: I've got to go.

VAL: Go after tea.

JOE: I'm going.

Exit JOE.

LEN: You can't not have toilets, you've got to have toilets – that theatre's the biggest begging bowl out.

DENNIS: Besides that hotel falling in the sea, it's what this town is famous for.

LEN: And who's paid for it?

VAL: He always has to go.

DENNIS: Any other town would welcome having a world-famous theatre.

LEN: So what's it doing here then?

DENNIS: I don't know.

LEN reads his paper.

VAL: He always has to go. Mothers and sons.

LEN: Aye. What about you Mister Wilson, how do you get on with your mother?

DENNIS: She died when I was very young.

VAL: Oh, you probably feel very close to your father then.

DENNIS: No. He left shortly after. He was a travelling salesman, he travelled in ladies underwear and drove a Morris Oxford, that's all I know.

VAL: Len worked in the travelling retail industry.

LEN: Kitchenware.

VAL: Until his operation.

LEN: The blokes in lingerie were always a bit fly by night.

VAL: I'll put your tea on, we'll have roast potatoes and mash.

Exit VAL.

LEN: You keep your hands off my sister.

DENNIS: She's old enough to be my mother.

LEN: You don't know what she's like.

DENNIS: That's no way to talk about your sister.

LEN: She's my sister.

Pause.

DENNIS: What sort of car did you drive as a salesman?

LEN: Watch it you, you've got no rights in this house, you're a guest. You're here at my say so, I could have you out at the drop of a hat – I'll be glad to see the back of you – you've got no rights, you're a guest.

DENNIS: I pay the rent.

LEN: No you don't, the bloody government does and I don't need your money – you're only here because she likes you.

DENNIS: So you never drove a Morris Oxford.

LEN: Coming in here, telling us we should have theatres instead of toilets. No self-respecting man, what self-respecting man – I couldn't live like it, I couldn't live with myself – it's a disgrace – no self-respecting man would let it happen – it's a disgrace, an outright disgrace – you're a parasite.

DENNIS: You don't want me to pay the rent then.

Enter VAL.

She gives DENNIS a plate with a large slice of cake on it.

VAL: Christmas cake.

DENNIS: Thank you.

LEN: Where's my cake?

VAL: You don't need any cake.

LEN: Neither does he.

VAL: He's a big lad, he needs feeding up.

LEN: What about me?

VAL: You eat too much Christmas cake.

LEN: I like Christmas cake.

VAL: That's the last bit.

DENNIS: Have some of mine if you like.

VAL: You leave the boy alone, let him eat his cake in peace.

LEN: I don't want his cake, I never asked for his cake.

VAL: You enjoy it.

DENNIS: I will.

VAL: I'll get you a glass of Dandelion and Burdock.

Exit VAL.

DENNIS: Have some cake if you like.

LEN: I don't want any of your cake thankyou very much.

DENNIS shovels cake into his mouth and LEN reads the paper.

Enter VAL with large glass of Dandelion and Burdock. She places the glass next to DENNIS.

VAL watches DENNIS eat.

VAL: I always sleep better knowing it's clean under my bed. You get worms if it's not. You get worms from the dust. You do, I'm telling you. I'm only saying. It's for your own good I'm telling you.

DENNIS: (*Mouth full.*) Mmmmh.

VAL: I made it myself.

DENNIS: Mmmmh.

LEN: (*Reading from paper.*) Mandy's sordid affair with the evil Glover, changed her from a bubbly outgoing housewife into a crazed bisexual, who killed her lesbian lover in a desperate bid to hold onto her milkman Svengali.

DENNIS drinks the glass of Dandelion and Burdock in one go.

VAL: Would you like some more?

LEN: Mister Wilson is thinking of leaving us Valerie.

VAL: But you've only just arrived.

LEN: He's going to New York.

DENNIS: Am I?

LEN: Yes.

VAL: What will you do for a hair dryer?

DENNIS: I've been before.

VAL: You'll have to buy a pair of Hush Puppies, to walk round New York in. Is it clean?

DENNIS: Very clean.

VAL: Would I like it?

DENNIS: Yes you would.

VAL: Have some more cake.

LEN: It's not clean.

VAL: It's clean.

LEN: You wouldn't like it, it's filthy dirty. Bloody Yanks. Winston Churchill was half Yank. What about you, have you got any Yank blood in you?

DENNIS: No.

LEN: You've got Yank blood in you.

VAL: There's Battenburg if you want.

DENNIS: No, no thanks, I'm full.

LEN: I'll have some Battenburg.

VAL: Oh, go on.

LEN: I wouldn't go to America if you paid me.

DENNIS: I'd like to go to New York.

VAL: You'd have to take an adaptor.

LEN: There's only one thing wrong with Europe – that's the French and the Germans.

VAL: Or there's lemon sponge cake.

LEN: I don't like America, I don't like Americans.

VAL: How would you know, you've never been. He doesn't go anywhere. It's been a great disappointment to us all that he hasn't travelled more. You're not wearing any socks.

DENNIS: No, I've lost them.

VAL: How can you lose your socks, you were wearing them when you went out.

DENNIS: I took them off, my feet were hot, and I left them on a bus.

VAL: The things people find on buses.

LEN: I've got as much chance of winning the Lottery as having my legs blown off.

Enter JOE.

JOE puts on his coat.

Where have you been?

JOE: I can't find my keys.

VAL: What's that you've got on?

JOE: Aftershave.

VAL: Where have you been?

JOE: In the bathroom.

VAL: What have you been doing in the bathroom?

JOE: I can't find my keys.

LEN: Life is boring.

VAL: What have you got aftershave on for?

JOE: I'm going for a drink.

VAL: You never used to drink.

LEN: He's always liked a drink.

VAL: He never used to drink, he never drank before he
went off with her, with that woman.

LEN: It is, it's boring.

VAL: He liked a drink but he never drank, and now he
drinks – you're an alcoholic, because of her.

JOE: Where have you put my keys?

VAL: I haven't touched your keys. You're not a man, you're
a husk – she snaps her fingers and you jump, you jump –
she says fetch and you go, tail wagging, grateful to be let
in the door while she carries on with some man behind
your back – it breaks my heart, you're not a man.

JOE: I know what I am, I'll tell you what I am – I'm
your son, your son – my mother's son – you made
me, you made me what I am, I'm your son, I'm my
mother's son.

Exit JOE.

LEN: You can't just – you've never learnt have you – you
can't just keep it shut, you have to make everyone's life
a misery.

Exit LEN.

DENNIS: I'll get a glass of Dandelion and Burdock.

VAL: It's his wife – she's got him wrapped round her little
finger. The first time it happened I made up a bed,
but I never heard, not a word – and I lay awake nights
thinking he was dead, face down in a gutter, a ditch, by
a road somewhere, and I nearly died with worry – to lose
a child... to think he's dead somewhere, to have your son
buried in the cold earth – and I wanted to know where

the grave was, so I could put some flowers on it.
The world is cruel, wicked and cruel.

I eat liver, I like liver.

DENNIS: I'll make you some tea.

VAL: No, no – it's very kind – I'm alright, it's alright,
I'll make the tea – you don't know the kitchen.

DENNIS: I don't mind.

VAL: You're a very kind boy.

DENNIS: You need a cup of tea.

VAL: I do, I do, I need a cup of tea. I can't, I really can't –
I can't go on any more.

DENNIS: I'll make some tea.

VAL: Yes.

Exit DENNIS.

VAL cries.

Enter DENNIS with bottle of Dandelion and Burdock.

DENNIS: I've put the kettle on.

VAL: You found it.

DENNIS: Yes.

Pours a large glass of Dandelion and Burdock and drinks it in one.

I know that something good or bad is happening, that
it's about to happen and that I'm not where I should
be... I forget everything – years, people, days... gone,
dissolved... trembling – the walls close in... my heart
trembles – I sit, I smoke, I stand, walking with fear,
shaking, every breath is my last – each cigarette lasts
a lifetime, an eternity to smoke – I don't smoke –

the fear, I get the fear and there's nothing – it's all nothing and I cling on for the light, if it's still the same, if it hasn't gone – in the morning, in the cold clear light of day... dissolving – every day and I feel like a foreigner... I can't remember.

VAL: I can't remember anything. It's no good trying, I've tried. I can read a book and enjoy reading it but I won't remember. You can't make yourself remember if you can't, can you. I blame it on the carving knife I had stuck in my head as a child. My mother threw a carving knife over the kitchen when I was a child and it stuck in my head. I walked round for hours with a bread knife stuck in my head. I don't really remember.

DENNIS: It's alright when I'm lying down. I lie awake at night with my eyes open... a loving mother, a loving father, a loving woman to wrap their arms around me... in the end I wrap my arms around myself... and I start praying... "Oh dear Lord"... "Please dear Lord" – and I can't get up and I think everything would be alright if only I was dead and I don't want to die and then I get up. I can't think of anyone.

VAL: When dad died – I didn't want him to see me cry and I couldn't think what to say and I just sat by his bed... and when it was time to go I kissed him on the forehead and said "Say hello to mam for me", and I felt stupid – all the dead people I know in Heaven are looking down at me and laughing.

DENNIS: You're not stupid.

VAL: I am, I'm stupid.

DENNIS: No you're not.

VAL: I am.

DENNIS: No.

VAL: I just wanted to know where his grave was, my son's grave... just thinking about it...

DENNIS puts his arm round her and comforts her.

He strokes her hair.

DENNIS: I bet you were a very attractive young girl. A very very attractive girl.

VAL: Oh Mister Wilson.

DENNIS: Dennis.

VAL: Mister Wilson.

DENNIS: Dennis.

VAL: Dennis.

DENNIS: Now you say it.

VAL: I'm old enough to be your mother.

DENNIS: Tell me you're a very attractive woman.

VAL: Mister Wilson.

DENNIS: Dennis. Say it.

VAL: I'm... I am...

DENNIS: Yes.

VAL: I am – a very... I can't.

DENNIS: Of course you can.

VAL: I am...

DENNIS: A very –

VAL: A very –

DENNIS: Attractive woman.

VAL: Attractive woman.

DENNIS: That's right.

VAL: Oh Dennis.

She kisses him.

Enter LEN with a bag of nails.

She pulls herself off DENNIS.

LEN: Bye it's froid. Right froid. That's French.

VAL: What would you like for tea Mister Wilson?

LEN: Right froid. We're having stew. Bugger for some. Now't we can do about it. Get thee sen some thick underwear, long johns, that's what I do. Fishermen have got it worse. It's like New York.

VAL: Oh yes, New York.

LEN picks up a hammer.

LEN: The weather's very much like New York.

VAL: Like New York.

Exit VAL.

DENNIS: So, you're going to do some banging then?

Silence.

You like banging, don't you?

Silence.

I'll go and lie down then.

Lie down on my bed, while you do your banging.

I might listen to some music.

She's nice your sister, I like your sister.

DENNIS goes to exit.

You'll need a bigger hammer than that.

Exit DENNIS.

LEN throws the bag of nails down hard at the floor.

End of act one.

ACT TWO

Scene 5

STEVEN.

Enter JOE from kitchen.

JOE: She's asleep.

STEVEN: She's been waiting up for you.

> *JOE throws box of matches at STEVEN. STEVEN ducks.*

STEVEN: Here, I like that pub.

JOE: Yeah.

STEVEN: I haven't been in a pub with just blokes like that for years. It was great.

JOE: Yeah.

STEVEN: I'm fed up of having to stare at women, years of staring at women in pubs and getting no response.

JOE: You just have to stare in there and you get a response.

STEVEN: I didn't stare at anyone.

JOE: No.

STEVEN: No, I didn't – I did not.

JOE: So what did that fella come over for then?

STEVEN: I didn't stare, it was just a glance.

JOE: And he came over.

STEVEN: That's why I looked at you.

JOE: Well I don't fancy you.

STEVEN: I don't fancy you neither.

JOE: You're an ugly bugger.

STEVEN: It's not me that's ugly mate.

JOE: You're ugly.

STEVEN: You're ugly.

JOE: No I'm not.

STEVEN: Yes you bloody are.

JOE: I'm not.

STEVEN: You are.

JOE: I'm not.

STEVEN: You are.

JOE: Right.

JOE pushes STEVEN.

STEVEN: Right.

STEVEN pushes JOE.

JOE: Right.

JOE pushes STEVEN.

They fight.

Enter VAL.

They stop fighting.

VAL: I fell asleep on the kitchen table.

JOE: You were waiting up.

VAL: No I wasn't. Where have you been?

JOE: The Star, up by Saint Mary's, just down from the castle.

VAL: I know where the Star is thank you very much.

STEVEN: It was his idea, I didn't want to go.

JOE: The barmen do a cocktail show every Thursday.

VAL: Your sister's not back then.

JOE: (*Shouts out back.*) Shirley!

No.

VAL: I'm going to bed.

JOE: Night then.

STEVEN: Night auntie Val.

Exit VAL.

JOE: Don't call her auntie Val.

STEVEN: I can call her it if I want.

JOE: She's not your bloody auntie.

STEVEN: Alright man, cool it, cool it.

Both sit and take out a beer.

JOE: I remember when all we had was a Chinese.

STEVEN: And now we've got everything.

JOE: Yeah.

They both open their beer.

Cheers.

STEVEN: Cheers.

They drink.

Chinese, Indian, McDonalds, the lot.

Enter DENNIS with mug.

Dracula.

DENNIS: I just want some water.

STEVEN: How about a drop of blood.

JOE: Tell Dennis your story Steven, go on – he'll like it, you'll like it.

DENNIS: Will I?

JOE: Yes.

STEVEN: What story?

JOE: We were in this club right – the Underground –

STEVEN: Oh yeah, yeah and there's this bird –

JOE: And she's all in leather.

STEVEN: Leather boots, leather skirt, leather bra –

JOE: And she grabs him.

STEVEN: She grabs hold of me, like this right, on the dance floor, on the fucking dance floor –

Enter SHIRLEY.

SHIRLEY: What are you grinning at?

STEVEN: Nothing.

SHIRLEY: I saw you, I saw you with that tart last night – she's a right tramp.

SHIRLEY puts handbag on table.

STEVEN: What do you care?

SHIRLEY: I don't.

JOE: How's it going then, sis?

SHIRLEY: I'm not talking to you, I'm not talking to any of you.

STEVEN: What about him – eh up Vamps, it's dark outside, about time you were off out in search of vestal virgins.

DENNIS: Yeah.

STEVEN: He hasn't got a reflection neither.

SHIRLEY: Steven!

STEVEN: What?

SHIRLEY: Dressed up like a dog's dinner, all in leather and she still couldn't pull a fella, so she had to take you home instead.

STEVEN: Oooooh.

SHIRLEY: What d'you have to come to my club for anyway?

STEVEN: Because we felt like it.

JOE: It's not your club, you don't own it.

SHIRLEY: The club where I work.

STEVEN: It's a free country.

SHIRLEY: And I don't like having to watch my older brother trying to cop off with school girls.

JOE: I never.

SHIRLEY: Who asked you to say anything?

JOE: What have I done?

SHIRLEY: Nothing.

Exit SHIRLEY.

STEVEN: So we get a cab right, back to her place, up off Eastgate – and there's this fat bloke right, sat in her front room, in front of the telly stuffing his face with Chinese and he doesn't say a word – he just sits watching the telly and there's nothing on, it's not even switched on, he's just staring at a blank telly.

JOE: And she kisses him on the head.

STEVEN: Yeah, yeah.

JOE: He's her husband.

STEVEN: So we go up to her room right and there's these horns, these massive great bloody horns on the wall over her bed, with a whip wrapped round them, a bull whip.

JOE: And then she – tell him, tell him.

STEVEN: She tells me to make a cup of tea.

DENNIS: What did you do?

JOE: He made her a cup of tea.

STEVEN: She had a kettle in her room. Are you listening or what?

JOE: Yeah.

DENNIS: Then what happened?

JOE: They drank the tea.

STEVEN: She lay on the bed face down, her head in the pillow moaning on and on and she tells me to whip her and I –

JOE: You never.

STEVEN: I did.

JOE: Liar.

STEVEN: I did, I whipped her.

JOE: He never, you never.

STEVEN: You get me a whip and a bird and I'll show you.

Pause.

77

DENNIS: So what was she like?

STEVEN: Alright, she looked alright.

JOE: Yeah, in the dark.

STEVEN: I woke up in the morning and she looked like my mam.

STEVEN and JOE laugh.

DENNIS: But what was she like?

STEVEN: She wasn't very friendly.

JOE: No, he wants to know what she was like.

STEVEN: Oh right, yeah, well she were – you know, like –

Holds his hands up searching for the right expression and unconsciously lowers them in front of his chest, hands cupped on either side as if weighted with flesh, as he hits on the right expression, and his hands shake with excitement.

– pretty – very, very, pretty.

DENNIS: Are you going to see her again?

STEVEN: Yeah.

Enter SHIRLEY. STEVEN doesn't see her.

You know what I wish, I wish I could just shag all my mates – like I could give you a right good seeing to and then we could watch match of the day and drink a load of beers.

SHIRLEY: Why don't you then?

STEVEN: Yeah, well – because I can't – I'm stood in the wrong queue for that, aren't I.

SHIRLEY: And what about that girl the other night?

STEVEN: What girl?

SHIRLEY: Not you, him.

JOE: What girl?

SHIRLEY: Bloody hell, her from Filey – you were old enough to be her dad.

JOE: Oh, her. It was nothing. I was drunk, she had a black mini skirt on and invited me back to her pub.

STEVEN: Was she married?

SHIRLEY: Who asked you to say anything?

STEVEN: Nobody.

SHIRLEY: Where are you going?

DENNIS: To get some water.

SHIRLEY: Right.

Exit DENNIS.

JOE: How could I say no, she came in a black mini skirt with a pub.

STEVEN: Two essential qualifications.

SHIRLEY: You're old enough to be her dad.

JOE: She said 'Do you want to come back to my pub for a drink.' All the time I kept looking at her thinking how much she must look like her dad.

STEVEN: You know her dad.

JOE: No – I just kept thinking she must look like him.

SHIRLEY: You can't just go round fucking any one you want when you want where you want, without thinking without caring.

STEVEN: Why not?

SHIRLEY: Because you can't.

JOE: I'm never going to see her again.

SHIRLEY: You are, you're old enough to be her bloody dad. Somebody will do that to your daughter one day – some old man will have her and then you'll know what it's like.

JOE: Thanks.

SHIRLEY: They will, I'm telling you.

JOE: I'll kill him.

STEVEN: It's only you Shirley, it's only you that I want.

SHIRLEY: Is that why you slept with someone else while we were still going out.

STEVEN: It didn't mean anything, I hardly knew her.

SHIRLEY: Thanks, thanks a bunch. You did it in front of my face – you said you loved me, you said you were going home to bed, and then you went off and fucked her.

JOE: Shirley.

SHIRLEY: He did it under my bloody nose.

STEVEN: I didn't mean it, I didn't know what I was doing.

SHIRLEY: You didn't know you had your hand up her skirt?

STEVEN: Yeah – no, it was an accident – I was, it was just – I was in the moment, I acted in the moment.

SHIRLEY: Oh give us a break. Did you wear a condom?

JOE: I'll put the kettle on.

SHIRLEY: You stay where you are.

JOE: I feel bad.

STEVEN: Why, what have you done?

SHIRLEY: Well.

STEVEN: What?

SHIRLEY: Did you?

STEVEN: Did I what?

SHIRLEY: Did you use a condom?

STEVEN: Yeah.

SHIRLEY: No you didn't.

STEVEN: I did.

SHIRLEY: You didn't.

STEVEN: I did.

SHIRLEY: You bloody didn't.

STEVEN: Alright, so I didn't.

JOE: I feel really bad now.

STEVEN: Yeah.

JOE: I was old enough to be her dad.

STEVEN: I don't know where my head is man, I don't know where the fuck it is, I don't know. I'm stupid.

SHIRLEY: You're not stupid.

STEVEN: Don't, I feel bad.

JOE: Stop it, the pair of you.

SHIRLEY: You're not stupid, you're not bad.

STEVEN: I feel bad.

SHIRLEY: You're a soft bastard.

STEVEN: Ah, don't say that.

He takes her hand.

SHIRLEY: Get off.

STEVEN: Come on.

SHIRLEY: Get off will you.

STEVEN: Kiss me. All I want is a kiss, I'm not going to shag you.

SHIRLEY slaps him across the face.

Exit SHIRLEY.

Shirley. You forgot your handbag.

STEVEN sits and drinks.

I love pornography, I think it's great it's the nearest you can get to sex without having sex, it's like sex itself without having to do it, it's great I love it.

JOE: I feel bad.

STEVEN: Why, what have you done?

JOE: Nothing.

STEVEN: I'm charmed me, I've got a charmed life.

JOE: Yeah.

STEVEN: Even the teachers at school said I was their favourite, even though I was a bloody nightmare – I totally charmed them.

JOE: Yeah, right.

STEVEN: You're just jealous.

JOE: I kept thinking he must be a lorry driver.

STEVEN: Who?

JOE: Her dad.

STEVEN: Whose dad?

JOE: That young girl with the pub, the one that
    I fucked.

STEVEN: What, you know her dad?

JOE: Oh, forget it.

STEVEN: Women. I want them all.

JOE: That's because you don't like any of them.

STEVEN: Watch it, eh.

JOE: Yeah?

STEVEN: Yeah.

    I'll bat thee one if tha doesn't watch it.

JOE: Oh, aye?

STEVEN: Aye.

    JOE cuffs STEVEN over head.

    I'll have you, I will.

JOE: Come on, I'll buy you a pint.

STEVEN: In the backyard, now.

JOE: You'd never come back in.

    STEVEN punches JOE.

    Get off.

STEVEN: Come on, come on.

    They scrap playfully.

JOE: Stop it will you.

STEVEN: Come on, fight like a man.

JOE: Stop tickling will you. Last one to the bar of the
    Central Hotel is a girl.

Exit JOE.

STEVEN: Hang on, that's not fair I wasn't ready.

Exit STEVEN.

Enter DENNIS.

DENNIS sits at table and rolls a cigarette.

Enter SHIRLEY.

DENNIS: They've gone.

SHIRLEY: I forgot my handbag.

DENNIS: Yeah.

SHIRLEY: I've always liked this room. It's cosy. It's the warmest in the house. I'm sorry about all that – me and Steven.

DENNIS: Oh.

SHIRLEY: He gets on my nerves.

DENNIS: Yeah.

SHIRLEY: Him and my brother – Oh, don't get me wrong, I like my brother.

DENNIS: Yeah, he's alright.

SHIRLEY: I love my brother.

DENNIS: Yeah.

SHIRLEY: I love all my family.

DENNIS: Yeah.

Silence.

DENNIS: Would you like to go for a drink?

SHIRLEY: When?

DENNIS: When would you like?

SHIRLEY: I don't know.

DENNIS: Next week.

SHIRLEY: Yeah.

DENNIS: You'd like that?

SHIRLEY: Yeah, oh yeah.

DENNIS: We'll have a laugh.

SHIRLEY: Right.

She picks up her handbag.

SHIRLEY: I left it in the back of a taxi last week.

DENNIS: What did you do that for?

SHIRLEY: It was an accident. I keep losing things. They
    don't approve of my new boyfriend. I only like this place
    in the summer. I could kill them. I'm saving up to go
    round the world. When Steven and I first stopped going
    out he kept ringing up to see how I was doing – to see
    I was alright, that I was coping, to say he missed me,
    how much he missed me, that he missed me so much he
    was thinking of getting a dog – I can't just leave, I can't
    just get up and go, I can't... I once went on a package
    holiday to Jamaica for a fortnight, a winter break in the
    sun and I had a great time – I felt free, really free –
    and then I came back and they'd done nothing – all
    the washing piled up in the hall, all their washing and
    cleaning and I did it and I didn't care, I'd been away –
    she can't manage without me... I bet you've travelled
    all over the world.

DENNIS: A bit, here and there, you know.

SHIRLEY: One day I will, I'll just go, pack up my bags and
    go without saying a word.

85

DENNIS: You'd better get a move on then.

SHIRLEY: You what?

DENNIS: There won't be much left to see soon.

SHIRLEY: Yeah, right.

DENNIS: Yeah.

SHIRLEY: Yeah.

DENNIS: Yeah. We're raping the planet burning up the planet and the planet's going mad – global warming, flowers budding in winter, melting ice caps rising sea levels, the wholesale destruction of rain forests, slash and burn – we're bleeding the planet dry and for what – Oil, oil and beefburgers – the rest of the world starves so we can ride around in fast cars stuff our faces with junk food and get a quick suntan.

SHIRLEY: Did you go to university?

DENNIS: College.

SHIRLEY: I thought you went to university?

DENNIS: College.

SHIRLEY: So, you wouldn't like it if I bought you a sports car?

DENNIS: No. The need the urge to destroy to usurp to procreate, and for what – there's no proof, none of it can be proved, only ourselves – there's a good breast there's a bad breast, yeah, I want to kill my father so I can sleep with my mother, I punish my mother because she betrayed me and slept with my father, yeah yeah – it's about money, it's about greed and anyone says different is a liar – people... they're all so, so – at it, at it all the time, up here – well I don't have to live in their heads, I don't have to have their conversations, I don't have to live in their universe...

SHIRLEY: Yeah, I get like that – well, no it's nothing like that – I keep having this dream that I'm out in space in a space suit – working on the spaceship right – and my thing gets cut and I'm drifting out into space and nothing can stop me – like going on forever into the blackness, getting sucked into the blackness.

Silence.

Do you always get this angry?

DENNIS: It's our fucking planet, it belongs to all of us.

SHIRLEY: I once thought about adopting a whale. Where are you going after this?

DENNIS: I don't know. Somewhere hot.

SHIRLEY: I bet you look nice in shorts. You've got lovely hands. Show me your hands. Go on. I can read hands. Go on.

He gives her his hand. She turns it over and looks at his palm, tracing the lines with her finger.

Oh, you've got a long life line – you're going to have two and a half children and never get married. And have many lovers. That's your mound of Venus. And you're going to travel a lot – I've never been anywhere, I just read about places in magazines – far away hot exotic places – You have, you've got nice hands.

She holds her hand up against his.

She kisses him.

The telephone rings.

SHIRLEY: You're bad.

She kisses him.

DENNIS pulls away.

87

Leave it.

She kisses him.

You're a bad boy.

They kiss.

I've got a boyfriend, a beautiful boyfriend. He's married.

He kisses her.

The telephone stops.

You're bad. You're a bad boy.

They kiss.

DENNIS pulls away.

What's the matter.

DENNIS: I can't. Bloody phone.

SHIRLEY: Why can't you.

DENNIS: I can't.

Enter VAL.

VAL: Mister Wilson.

DENNIS: Yes.

VAL: Do you pull the blind down when you have a shower.

DENNIS: No.

VAL: You can see right through the glass, I've been in the backyard to look through several times.

Pause.

There's a phone call.

SHIRLEY: I'm going to get a lock put on my bedroom door.

VAL: What for.

SHIRLEY: Privacy, I've got a right to privacy.

VAL: Not in my house you don't. There's a phone call for you Mister Wilson. It's gone midnight. You can take it in the hall.

Exit DENNIS.

VAL: Oh, I never told you did I.

SHIRLEY: What?

VAL: I never told you.

SHIRLEY: What, what?

VAL: I saw Rosemary Tredwell the other day, in the car park.

SHIRLEY: What car park?

VAL: Outside Tescos. She pulled up and got out with her husband.

SHIRLEY: You what?

VAL: With her husband.

SHIRLEY: She's got a husband?

VAL: Yes, a husband.

SHIRLEY: What, she's married?

VAL: Yes.

SHIRLEY: She's got a husband?

VAL: Yes.

SHIRLEY: When did she get married?

VAL: I don't know.

SHIRLEY: How do you know it's her husband then?

VAL: She told me.

SHIRLEY: She told you?

VAL: Yes, she told me.

SHIRLEY: Alright, I'm only asking.

VAL: And she's going to have a baby.

Enter DENNIS.

SHIRLEY goes to leave.

Where are you going?

SHIRLEY: To get married – my boyfriend has asked me to marry him, we're engaged to be married.

VAL: He'll have to get divorced first.

SHIRLEY: I'm going out, I'm going out to get pregnant.

Exit SHIRLEY.

VAL: Are you alright?

DENNIS: Yes.

VAL: Everything's alright?

DENNIS: Yes.

VAL: There's nothing wrong?

DENNIS: No.

VAL: Nothing bad's happened? I thought it might be serious – ringing this time of night.

DENNIS: I'm sorry, it won't happen again.

VAL: He said he was ringing from a phone box, he said it was urgent, he said he was ringing from Scotland.

DENNIS: Yeah. He's a friend, an old friend.

It wasn't anything.

VAL: Would you like some hot chocolate?

DENNIS: No, thank you, no.

VAL: I had a dream about you last night, I dreamed you
were walking round the house in flannelette pyjamas.
I don't suppose you wear pyjamas.

DENNIS: No.

VAL: Just like Len, all he wears is a tee shirt and shorts.
What do you wear?

DENNIS: Nothing, I don't wear anything.

VAL: When Len went in for his operation he wore hospital
pyjamas for weeks, it was embarrassing, he wouldn't
even let me buy him a pair of slippers. I bought him
a beautiful cotton dressing gown and he refused to wear
it. I don't suppose you've got a dressing gown either.

DENNIS: Yes – yeah, I do.

VAL: Oh, I haven't seen you wearing it.

You should wear it round the house, save you getting
dressed in the mornings.

Just get out of bed and slip into your dressing gown.

DENNIS: Right.

VAL: I'll get you a pair of slippers.

We hardly wore anything when I was young – string
vests, big belts and short skirts walking up and down the
front. Are you warm enough like that?

DENNIS: Two jumpers and a shirt.

VAL: Good boy. I have to make sure everyone's warm
enough. Just a string vest and barely nothing else.

DENNIS: He was like a father to me.

VAL: You've got a scar under your chin as well.

DENNIS: I fell as a child.

VAL: Just like Paul.

DENNIS: They had to sew it back on.

VAL: He's got scars in exactly the same places. Paul's my older brother. He was very protective of me as a young woman – if a man so much as looked at me he went mad.

DENNIS: I'm sorry about the phone call.

VAL: Oh, that's alright.

DENNIS: It won't happen again, I've told him not to do it again, I've told him not to ring again.

VAL: Any time up till ten's fine with me, except for emergencies.

DENNIS: Goodnight.

VAL: Goodnight Dennis.

Exit DENNIS.

Scene 6

VAL, LEN and JOE.

VAL reading a letter.

VAL: Your uncle Paul's fed up of the winter and his neighbours have gone to live in Australia.

LEN: Why doesn't he write to me?

VAL: Now your cousin's in jail he's back to himself again... (*Reads.*) "He's a nice boy. It's the drugs. I just hope he can't afford to buy any while he's locked up. I don't hold out much hope though. When he gets out it's back here and all his mates. They all do it. I don't have much hope for him."

LEN: He never writes to me.

VAL: He's been made captain of the pub quiz team.

LEN: Oh, a big responsibility.

VAL: Don't talk about your own brother like that.

LEN: He's a big head.

VAL: You've never forgiven him for passing the eleven plus.

LEN: His head's so big he can't get it through the door.

JOE: Oooh.

LEN: Why aren't you working?

JOE: I'm not well.

VAL: Don't look at me.

JOE: I'm sick.

VAL: I've got no sympathy.

LEN: I used to drink ten pints a night – fifteen at the weekend, and never missed a day's work and I had a proper job.

JOE: And pickled your liver – Oooh.

VAL: They had to rush your cousin's baby into hospital last week – it couldn't breathe.

JOE: Mmmmh.

VAL: Poor little kiddie – that's the second time and it was only born in July.

JOE: What cousin's this?

VAL: That's three he's got now, one from her previous husband and two of his own. They don't know what's got into the little boy, he's only two and keeps kicking

and biting and throttling his little sister and she's
only one – it got so bad they had to shout at him so
hard he hid under a table all day, but he still came
back and did it again. Your auntie thinks he's trying
to murder her. Mind you, his father was a bit funny –
he took Tanya's hand one day spread it out flat
pinned to the bread board and chopped off the top
of her index finger with a breadknife cussing. Well
that's what she says. He never comes round to see
the boy. Not like you and your wife.

JOE: We never got married.

LEN: How's Mister Big?

VAL: You still love your wife.

JOE: (*Looking at LEN.*) I'd like to break her neck and kick
her down the stairs.

VAL: You love her.

JOE: I don't love her.

VAL: You love her.

JOE: No.

VAL: Why do you want to kick her down the stairs?

LEN: How can you tell if someone's in disguise, how do
you know that isn't them?

VAL: You love your wife.

JOE: No I don't – she says I don't care and I don't, she's
right I don't – she's miserable, it's not my fault she's
miserable I didn't make her miserable.

VAL: You must have done something.

JOE: Whatever I did was never enough, never good
enough, never enough – not for her, not for the baby,

not for anything – so she ran off with some bloody
errand boy, fetching this carrying that, and now she
wants to bleed me dry – I'd like to kick her down the
stairs and break her neck – she's the one person in the
world I'd pay to have killed.

LEN: Only the one – I could fill a supermarket.

JOE: I could, I could have her killed – it's what she tells the
baby that worries me – don't you dare, don't, don't –
don't even think it.

VAL: What, think what – what am I thinking?

JOE: Just shut it. Right.

VAL: Right.

LEN: Does Mister Big have a beard?

VAL: Where did you get your hair cut?

LEN: Prospect Road.

VAL: You can't even do that, you're useless, you were born
like it.

LEN: What, what did I do?

JOE: I want to kick her down the stairs break her neck
and kill her.

VAL: I've never trusted a man with a beard, all that dirt
on his face.

LEN turns on the television.

LEN: I expect nothing, if you expect nothing then you can't
be disappointed.

VAL: Yes you can. I wish you never had to see that woman
again in your life – alright, alright I'm just saying.

JOE: Well don't.

VAL looks up at the television screen.

I won't let a woman tell me what to do with my money –
I won't, you hear me, I won't.

VAL: Is that a dark man or is he just dirty – oh no, he's got
black legs as well.

JOE: You're prejudiced.

VAL: I'm not afraid to admit it.

LEN: There's no one more prejudiced than the young, smug
and ignorant – where is your Mister Wilson?

VAL: He's not my Mister Wilson.

LEN: I haven't seen him, what does he do up there all day?

VAL: He's got his music.

LEN: I can't hear anything.

VAL: He's got earphones.

LEN: She thinks he looks like the man out of the catalogue.

JOE: If you were twenty years younger mam I'd
recommend you go out with him.

VAL: Oh, Joe.

Enter SHIRLEY.

And where were you last night?

SHIRLEY: Didn't you hear me come in? I slept in the front
room. I didn't want to wake anyone. It was late. You were
all asleep. I was drunk, I fell asleep on the settee.

JOE: You couldn't have.

SHIRLEY: I did.

JOE: I put the bolts across last night and then I unbolted
them when I got up this morning.

LEN: He was out early after Mister –

JOE: I'm warning you.

SHIRLEY: No, I put the bolts across after I came in.

JOE: Did you?

SHIRLEY: Yeah.

VAL: You spent the night with him, your adulterating lover.

SHIRLEY: I put the bolts across.

VAL: No you didn't, Joe bolted up before he went to bed –
    didn't you son?

JOE: I can't remember mam.

SHIRLEY: I came home last night.

VAL: You never.

SHIRLEY: I did.

VAL: You never.

JOE: What's it matter, she's a grown woman.

VAL: Out all night with a married man, and everyone said
    you were an angel.

SHIRLEY: I never, I came home.

VAL: No you didn't.

SHIRLEY: I did.

VAL: Joe put the bolts across.

SHIRLEY: He never.

JOE: I don't remember.

SHIRLEY: I came home.

VAL: You didn't.

SHIRLEY: I did – why won't you believe me.

VAL: You can't be trusted.

LEN: Somebody's lying.

SHIRLEY: No I'm not – nobody's lying.

LEN: Who's lying?

SHIRLEY: Nobody.

LEN: Your mother's lying?

SHIRLEY: I don't know – no.

LEN: Somebody must be – it didn't get like this for nothing.

SHIRLEY: Nobody's lying.

LEN: Someone's to blame – who's to blame – not me, it wasn't me, it's not my fault – some stupid soft bugger's to blame for all this.

Exit SHIRLEY.

VAL: She's breaking my heart.

JOE: Why can't you just leave her alone.

VAL: If I don't tell her who will, I'm her mother – just because I made a mess of my life doesn't mean she has to.

JOE: She's old enough to look after herself.

VAL: What do you know, you gave your child a rat for it's birthday.

JOE: No I never.

VAL: He gave her a rat.

JOE: It was from a friend.

VAL: One of her friends.

JOE: We didn't keep it.

VAL: No, you gave it to some other poor unfortunate child living in that squat.

JOE: It wasn't a squat.

VAL: It was a squat – they kept rats for pets.

JOE: We didn't keep it, we gave it to the community centre.

VAL: They lived in a squat.

JOE: It wasn't a squat, it was short life, it was a co-operative, it was a housing association.

VAL: They were all drug addicts.

JOE: Mam.

VAL: You left home and you went barmy.

JOE: Stop it will you – I'm going right, I'm going, I'm getting out – my head can't be doing with any of this – I had to go I couldn't stay, I had to – what did you want me to do – I was young.

LEN: We're all allowed to be young, when does it stop that's what I want to know.

VAL: It's all my fault, I blame myself.

JOE: For what, what for – how can you blame yourself, what do you blame yourself for – you can't blame yourself, I left home, I had to, I couldn't stay, I had to go.

VAL: You never got over your dad going away.

JOE: I don't even remember him, I was only a baby – I was a baby.

VAL: You loved your dad. You did. He loved you.

JOE: So how come he left?

VAL: He was a chef at the Golden Egg.

JOE: And that's why he left?

LEN: He couldn't cook, he was a scoundrel.

VAL: You used to wait for him to come round, every Saturday morning with his money – and then one day he didn't come, he stopped the money stopped and you've never been the same since.

JOE: I don't remember.

VAL: You were three.

LEN: Stop going on will you, I'm trying to watch the telly.

VAL: I blame myself.

JOE: What for?

VAL: Everything.

JOE: Don't, please mam, don't.

VAL: It's true.

JOE: No it's not, it's not true – don't say that.

LEN: Why not – it makes her feel better.

VAL: No it doesn't.

LEN: Then stop it.

Loud triumphal music from the television.

They all look at the television.

VAL: Turn it down, turn it down.

LEN turns the volume down.

You said it didn't work.

LEN: It doesn't.

TELEVISION: And now for a brief foray into the world of 'Working Principles', presented by –

The sound cuts out.

LEN tries to get the sound back.

LEN: Cheap foreign rubbish. I told you it didn't work.

VAL: What did he say it was about?

LEN: Working principles.

JOE goes to leave.

Oh aye, that's him off out the door, off down the pub, down the pub to look for Mister Big – buy him a pint from me.

Exit JOE.

The world's lost its sense of humour.

Enter SHIRLEY.

SHIRLEY: I'm going to work.

Silence.

There's nothing needs doing?

VAL: I'll just give the place a quick clean.

SHIRLEY: But there's nothing needs doing?

VAL: I'm just going to clean the house.

SHIRLEY: Yes I know, but what I'm saying is there's nothing needs doing.

VAL: Just the washing, the dishes –

SHIRLEY: But there's nothing needs doing.

VAL: You're going to work.

SHIRLEY: Alright, I'll do the dishes.

VAL: I don't want you to do the dishes.

SHIRLEY: You said they need doing.

VAL: It's alright, I'll do them.

SHIRLEY: No – if there are things to be done I'll do them, I'll do my fair share.

VAL: It's not important.

SHIRLEY: So there's nothing needs doing.

Just tell me.

VAL: I've told you.

SHIRLEY: There's nothing needs doing.

VAL: You're going to work.

Exit SHIRLEY.

VAL goes to leave.

VAL trips over a pot of paint.

VAL: This house is a death trap.

Exit VAL.

Scene 7

JOE, STEVEN and DENNIS.

JOE: She's not mad, she's not ill – lying, sad, unhappy, lonely, miserable, two-faced – I'm a drunk, I'm a liar, I let her down, I let her down – she wouldn't know a good turn if it turned round and slapped her in the face – I want to kill her. And now, and now – when I've finally been kissed awake and the scales have dropped away –

it's an illness, the way I think about her is an illness. She's sick and I feel better, I forgive her everything – it's an illness. She went off with another man and now he's left her I want her, I want to fuck her – I want to make everything all alright. It's an illness, I've got an illness, I'm sick.

Exit JOE.

STEVEN: I've given up beef.

DENNIS: What for?

STEVEN: Mad cow.

DENNIS: What about those?

STEVEN: What about them?

STEVEN drags on his cigarette.

Have you ever seen them kill a cow? It's horrible man. You can see it in their eyes, they know what's happening, they can smell death. You can feel the fear. Cows suffer. Cows have got feelings the same as you and me.

DENNIS: So what's the difference?

STEVEN: There isn't any.

DENNIS: Cows can't talk.

STEVEN: Yeah.

DENNIS: A cow can't say I am a cow but we can, that's the difference.

STEVEN: Yeah, but –

DENNIS: We've got consciousness.

STEVEN: A cow might not know it's a cow but that doesn't mean they don't talk to each other.

DENNIS: No, they don't talk, that's the point they can't. A cow can't say I am a cow.

STEVEN: No – but they've probably got another word for it in their own language, just because they don't talk in English doesn't mean they haven't got any conscience.

DENNIS: Consciousness.

STEVEN: Yeah, right.

DENNIS drinks a pint of water down in one.

Steady with the water Dennis you'll drown yourself.

DENNIS: I can't stop drinking.

STEVEN: What is your drink?

DENNIS: Water.

STEVEN: No, no – What's your drink?

DENNIS: Water.

STEVEN: No, but what do you like?

DENNIS: Water.

STEVEN: I know what you like, Bulls Blood.

STEVEN laughs.

Get it eh, Bulls Blood wine – for Vampires. Bulls Blood – Oh, forget it.

DENNIS drinks water.

DENNIS: I can't stop drinking, I'm thirsty all the time. I keep falling asleep, I'm tired all the time and I've started taking sugar in my tea.

STEVEN: Step inside my cannibal head man and I'll rip your fucking head off.

DENNIS: I can't wake up.

STEVEN: You want to see a doctor. Get him to look at your funny bone while you're at it.

STEVEN lights up a joint.

DENNIS: (*Sings.*) 'Let me take you down, 'cos we're going to Strawberry Fields.'

STEVEN: Here, can you juggle?

DENNIS: 'Strawberry Fields.'

STEVEN: I can juggle.

DENNIS: 'With nothing to get hung up about.'

STEVEN: Yeah.

Gives DENNIS the joint.

Exit STEVEN.

DENNIS: 'Strawberry Fields forever.'

DENNIS takes a long drag on the joint.

Enter STEVEN.

STEVEN: She's only got two eggs.

STEVEN juggles eggs with one hand. Full of brio and showmanship.

He throws one of the eggs high into the air, holds onto the other and steps forward so that the descending egg cracks open on his head.

Dah – Daaaaaaah!

STEVEN, with arms outstretched as if awaiting applause, holds his position. Finally his face cracks and he falls about laughing.

His laughter becomes hysterical. He tries to speak but can hardly get the words out.

The yolk – The yolk – The yolk – is – on me. Oh God...
it hurts – it hurts.

Recovers himself.

DENNIS: What did you do that for?

STEVEN takes joint.

STEVEN: Misery guts.

STEVEN can't stop laughing.

DENNIS: I lived in a house with no doorbell and no
telephone for a long time and I was happy.

STEVEN: What happened?

DENNIS: They kicked us out and declared it unfit for
human habitation.

STEVEN: Feel my leg.

DENNIS: I put a lot of physical energy into my room.

STEVEN: It's shaking.

DENNIS: I like it.

STEVEN: I can't stop my leg shaking.

DENNIS: I'm happy doing nothing.

STEVEN: Feel it. Just feel it – go on, feel it.

DENNIS feels STEVEN's leg.

That's my leg.

DENNIS: Yeah.

DENNIS lets go of STEVEN's leg.

I don't do nothing – I go round and round in my head
and I have to lie down.

STEVEN: What, are you sick or something?

DENNIS: No.

STEVEN: It's the daylight mate, you've been exposed to too much daylight, you're not used to it, you want to draw your curtains and get back in your box quick.

STEVEN closes his eyes.

DENNIS: I've been here before.

STEVEN: Oh, no.

DENNIS: You don't remember me then?

STEVEN: No.

DENNIS: I was small?

STEVEN: When.

DENNIS: I don't know. You don't remember. Before you were born.

STEVEN: We get a lot of visitors.

A smile creeps across STEVEN's face.

DENNIS: What, what, what you smiling at?

STEVEN: Nothing.

DENNIS: No, what, go on, what?

STEVEN's smile sets into a permanent grin.

She was a perfect reader, a perfect drawer. When she went through the doors of the hospice she said "I want to die here" and I asked why and she said "Because ever since I came through those doors there's been peace." She was on morphine twenty-four hours a day, no pain – it was beautiful the way she went. She had to write everything down towards the end – I've got everything she wrote from October to December. Two hundred pages – this size, both sides – and drawings, some of them don't make any sense – she'd say take a look at that, what do you think of that and I couldn't make head nor tail – it was the morphine, it did funny things, she was hallucinating towards the end. I wouldn't have wanted it any other way, it was beautiful. And some of the pages, you should see them – she's written this way and then this and then back again.

STEVEN: She's gyrating.

DENNIS: Who's gyrating?

STEVEN: This girl.

DENNIS: What girl?

STEVEN: The girl in my head. She's gyrating.

DENNIS: Yeah.

STEVEN: Yeah. Gyrating in a backwards direction and from side to side thrusting forwards on the beat with her pelvis.

DENNIS: What's she like?

STEVEN: Yeah – she's pretty.

Unaware, he gestures with his hands in front of his chest.

Very, very, pretty.

DENNIS: I'm hot.

STEVEN: Yeah.

DENNIS: It's hot.

STEVEN opens his eyes.

STEVEN: It was wonderful.

DENNIS: Yeah.

STEVEN: Yeah – I had a wonderful time.

DENNIS: I loved her.

STEVEN: We've got this telephonist at work – Ooooh – She's engaged, engaged to be married. You should see the rock he's given her.

DENNIS: It's hot.

STEVEN: It's so big right, you could charge people for taking them round it. They're getting married in March.

DENNIS: Are you hot?

STEVEN: He wants a baby.

DENNIS: I'm hot.

STEVEN: She's trying for a baby as soon as she can after the wedding, in the first nine months if not sooner – I offered to help her out.

DENNIS takes off his jumper.

Where are you going?

DENNIS: To open a window.

STEVEN: Don't open a window.

DENNIS: It's hot.

STEVEN: It's cold.

DENNIS: I'm hot.

STEVEN: Have a drink.

STEVEN takes out a flask of brandy.

I keep it for the car, it's medicinal, for emergencies – like if I get an hysterical woman or summat.

STEVEN gives flask to DENNIS.

DENNIS drinks.

Christmas.

DENNIS gives flask to STEVEN.

STEVEN drinks.

DENNIS takes out small ornate tin that looks like a snuff box.

DENNIS: My mother came from Chesterfield.

STEVEN: What's that for?

DENNIS: And my dad drove a Morris Oxford.

STEVEN: What do you keep in there.

DENNIS: Tablets.

STEVEN: Oh, aye?

DENNIS: It's empty.

STEVEN: The only tablets I like are the ones that make your head go pop.

DENNIS: They don't remember. No one remembers. I can't remember.

STEVEN: You what?

DENNIS: My dad.

STEVEN: Yeah, well.

Silence.

I love Shirley. I do – I do. I do. I'm going to marry her. I'm going to pick her up from work in my car and I'm going to tell her. What do you think?

DENNIS: Yeah.

STEVEN: You think I should?

DENNIS: Yeah.

STEVEN: You really think I should?

Right. That's what I'll do then.

I do I love her, I love her, I love Shirley.

STEVEN drinks the rest of the flask in one.

There's a drop left, finish it.

STEVEN goes to exit.

You haven't got any mints have you?

DENNIS: No.

Exit STEVEN.

DENNIS opens the window and takes off his shirt.

Takes large crumpled piece of paper out of pocket.

DENNIS picks up phone and dials number from paper.

Hello... hello... yeah, yeah... I needed to hear the sound of your voice... a voice, your voice... I need space – space – Yeah – I have... I have, I've missed you... I just want space... tomorrow, I'll ring tomorrow.

Puts phone down.

DENNIS picks up jumper shirt and flask of brandy.

DENNIS turns out the light.

Exit DENNIS.

Scene 8

VAL in black sat at a table.

A tobacco tin stuffed with cotton wool sits open in front of her.

She turns a small lock of cut hair between her fingers.

Silence.

Enter SHIRLEY.

SHIRLEY: I came as soon as I could.

She takes off her coat.

We were stocktaking. They've given me the day off.

Exit SHIRLEY with coat.

VAL lays the lock of hair on the cotton wool in the tobacco tin.

Enter SHIRLEY.

You're alone.

VAL: They've taken him up the hospital, Len's gone with him.

SHIRLEY lights a cigarette.

Can I have one?

SHIRLEY: You don't smoke.

VAL: Neither do you.

SHIRLEY gives VAL a cigarette.

SHIRLEY: Maybe it was something he ate.

VAL: We don't know. I need a light.

SHIRLEY: Oh, yeah.

SHIRLEY lights VAL's cigarette.

VAL: I'll get an ashtray.

Exit VAL.

SHIRLEY picks up the lock of hair and feels it.

Enter VAL with ashtray.

VAL watches SHIRLEY with lock of hair. As soon as SHIRLEY sees VAL watching she replaces the hair.

VAL puts ashtray on the table.

VAL: It's from Majorca.

SHIRLEY: What's that?

VAL: A tobacco tin.

SHIRLEY: Can I have another look?

VAL: If you like.

SHIRLEY takes out the lock of hair.

SHIRLEY: It's blond. Whose is it?

Joe's not blond. Was Joe blond?

VAL: No.

SHIRLEY: It's mine. I wasn't blond.

Whose is it?

VAL: It's best forgot.

VAL takes the lock of hair.

It's best forgot.

Enter LEN.

LEN: They've kept his body. For the postmortem. He went off into some sort of coma. He was diabetic. He'd been drinking and had too much sugar in his blood. They don't think he felt anything.

VAL: Poor boy.

LEN: Yes.

VAL puts lock of hair back in tin and puts the lid on.

What are you wearing black for?

VAL: Mister Wilson.

LEN: He's a stranger, he's died without paying his rent, he's left us with a bloody big headache and you get all dressed up for him.

SHIRLEY: You've got no compassion.

LEN: You pay the bills.

SHIRLEY: We'll have to tell his family.

LEN: They can settle his rent.

VAL: He's got a friend in Scotland but we don't have a number. We'll have to hope someone rings.

LEN: I'll go and look in his room.

SHIRLEY: You can't do that.

LEN: Why not?

SHIRLEY: He's dead.

LEN: So he won't mind then.

LEN goes to exit.

Do you think they pay compensation for this sort thing – the Council, the Government, the Social services – for the expense of it all – clearing up the mess, who'll pay for that. And then there's the detriment to business – who wants to sleep in a dead man's bed?

VAL: I took him up some porridge.

LEN: What were you doing giving him porridge in bed?

VAL: I knocked on the door but there wasn't any answer. As soon as I opened the door I knew he was dead. I could feel it.

LEN: Who's going to pay to have him buried? I'm not paying and that's for sure.

Exit LEN.

VAL: I'm being punished, God is punishing me.

SHIRLEY: You don't believe in God. Well you don't.
    You don't go to Church.

VAL: I was wicked and he's punishing me.

SHIRLEY: You're just upset that's all. We're all upset.

VAL: Every morning I wake up I look in the mirror and see
    this old woman, and I think there's been some terrible
    mistake, and if only I go back to bed and get a lot of
    sleep, I'll wake up again in the morning and it will all be
    alright. I keep washing my face and every time I look up
    again I think I'll be twenty-five again.

STEVEN: (*Offstage.*) It's alright auntie Val, it's only me.

VAL: I'll wash his sheets.

Enter STEVEN.

STEVEN: Bloody hell, what's happened – somebody died.

SHIRLEY: Mister Wilson.

STEVEN: You what?

SHIRLEY: Mister Wilson's dead.

STEVEN: No he's not.

SHIRLEY: He is Steven.

STEVEN: He's not.

SHIRLEY: You think I'm making it up?

STEVEN: No, he can't be – what happened, somebody drive a
    stake through his heart – I was drinking with him last night.

VAL: You were probably the last person to see him alive.

STEVEN: What, you mean he is – he's dead, really dead, like
    dead dead. Bloody hell. When did all this happen then?

SHIRLEY: Last night.

STEVEN: But I was with him last night – he was alright, he looked aright.

SHIRLEY: He went into a coma.

STEVEN: He kept saying he was hot. Bloody hell. I've never met anyone that's died before.

VAL: Oh, my feet.

VAL takes off her shoes and rubs feet.

STEVEN: Where did he die?

SHIRLEY: In his bed.

STEVEN: Where is he now?

SHIRLEY: The hospital.

VAL: My poor feet.

STEVEN: We're sat in the room under where he died.

VAL: Ooooh.

STEVEN: He died just on the other side of that ceiling.

SHIRLEY: Yeah.

VAL: We never had proper shoes as children.

JOE: (*Offstage.*) Come on then you buggers, you want it come and get it, I'll give it you alright.

Exit STEVEN.

Enter LEN with portable CD player.

VAL: What's the matter with Joe?

LEN: How should I know.

SHIRLEY: What's that?

LEN: What's it look like?

JOE: (*Offstage.*) Let me at the buggers, I'll kill the buggers.

VAL: There's something going on, what's going on?

SHIRLEY: That's not yours.

LEN: It is now.

SHIRLEY: Put it back.

LEN: What for?

JOE: (*Offstage.*) You've got no bloody balls, you've got no balls.

VAL: What's going on?

SHIRLEY: Put it back.

LEN: It's no good to him now.

VAL: God will punish you for this.

Exit VAL.

LEN: Let him. When has God ever helped me? God only helps the rich.

SHIRLEY: Put it back you hear, put it back – it's not yours.

LEN: Here, I found a number to ring, it was by his bed and there's a name.

LEN gives large piece of crumpled paper to SHIRLEY.

SHIRLEY: (*Reads.*) Bill.

LEN: Yeah, Bill.

SHIRLEY: Who's Bill?

LEN: How should I know.

Enter JOE with STEVEN and VAL.

JOE's face is bloody and his shirt torn.

JOE: It's alright mam, I can manage.

VAL: Get me a flannel, get me a flannel.

JOE: I'm alright, it's alright.

Exit SHIRLEY into kitchen.

JOE: I can manage, I don't need any help.

VAL: Sit down, sit down.

JOE sits.

STEVEN: He's been mugged.

LEN: When?

JOE: It's nothing.

LEN: They must have come from Leeds.

STEVEN: How do you know that?

LEN: There's no blacks live round here.

JOE: They weren't black.

Enter SHIRLEY with bowl of water and flannel.

Mam, I'm alright.

VAL: Sit still.

JOE: Mam.

VAL: Sit still.

VAL wrings out the flannel.

STEVEN: He looks prettier like that.

LEN: I'll ring the police.

JOE: No, no police, I don't want any police.

VAL wipes his face.

Ouch, that hurt.

STEVEN: But you've been mugged.

JOE: I don't want any police.

SHIRLEY: Mister Wilson's dead.

JOE: Yeah – I know.

SHIRLEY: You know?

JOE: I was here when mam found his body.

VAL: Keep still will you.

JOE: Mam.

VAL: Baby.

SHIRLEY: And you went out?

JOE: I had to, I had to go out. The world doesn't stop you know. She was alright – it was alright. Ouch. Give me that, give me the flannel mam.

He takes the flannel.

I can do it myself, I can manage on my own.

JOE gives his face a quick wipe.

VAL: You need a bath.

LEN: I spend most of my life thinking I'm going to die.

VAL: You are.

LEN: Today, tomorrow, the day after, three months, three years – sometime in the future, but soon.

VAL: You don't get off that easy.

STEVEN picks up CD player.

STEVEN: Whose is this?

SHIRLEY: Mister Wilson's.

STEVEN: What's it doing down here?

LEN: I was looking for an address, he said I could borrow it.

STEVEN: Bollocks.

LEN: He hasn't paid the rent.

JOE: So, when am I going to get a cup of tea?

SHIRLEY: We're in a state of shock.

VAL: You'll need to put a clean shirt on.

LEN picks up portable CD player.

SHIRLEY: Where are you going with that?

LEN: To put it in the shed.

SHIRLEY: You leave his belongings alone, you hear.

LEN: Yeah, yeah.

SHIRLEY: Leave his things where they belong.

LEN: I wasn't going to touch them.

VAL: So stay where you are then.

LEN puts down the portable CD and sits.

JOE: If I'd have had a gun, I'd have blown their heads off.

SHIRLEY: It's lucky for you that you didn't then.

JOE: They were from London.

LEN: Maybe they work for Mister Big.

STEVEN: Who's Mister Big?

Exit JOE.

VAL: I'll wash his sheets.

Exit VAL.

LEN: He's a bloody storyteller. It's the drugs I blame,
I blame all the drugs.

Exit LEN.

SHIRLEY opens the tobacco tin and looks at the lock of blond hair.

STEVEN: What's that?

SHIRLEY: Nothing.

SHIRLEY puts the lock of hair back in the tin and turns away.

STEVEN: What, what?

SHIRLEY: Nothing.

STEVEN: Shirley.

SHIRLEY: What?

STEVEN: Nothing. I got stopped for drink-driving last
night. I was coming to see you.

SHIRLEY: You were drunk.

STEVEN: No, I wasn't.

SHIRLEY: So why did they stop you?

STEVEN: I don't know – because they're police, because
they've got nothing better to do because they're pigs –
it was frosty I couldn't see, I turned left and I drove
up past Woolies on the footpath and there was this
copper stood outside Boots watching. I was going to
ask you to marry me.

SHIRLEY: You were drunk.

STEVEN: Alright, I'd had a couple, I was over the limit, but I wasn't drunk. Shirley –

He takes her arm but she pulls away.

SHIRLEY: Sometimes I think of the future – well, you know – like in the films, that it's already happened or it's already happening somewhere – that I'm already dead in the future somewhere, my life has already happened and I'm dead.

STEVEN: So you're already dead, you don't have to worry about dying.

SHIRLEY: I'm not. Like when you look at a star, you're not really seeing it, you're seeing it like it was millions of years ago – it might already be dead and you're still seeing it.

STEVEN: There's this bloke in America dedicated his whole life to perfecting the technique of time travel – he just can't get the mice to come back.

SHIRLEY laughs.

Well they must be going somewhere. Will you?

SHIRLEY: What? Steven. Look, please – don't, don't – what?

STEVEN: Because of him.

SHIRLEY: It's got nothing to do with him.

STEVEN: Your married man.

Exit SHIRLEY.

Enter LEN.

LEN: You're still here then.

STEVEN: Yeah.

LEN: Right.

Enter JOE with bag.

JOE: Where's my mam?

LEN: Upstairs cleaning out his room.

JOE: No she's not.

LEN: Here, there's a bloke out back looking for you – says his name's Mister Big.

JOE: You think it's funny don't you.

LEN: No, I don't.

STEVEN: Who's Mister Big?

JOE: No one.

STEVEN: So why talk about him?

JOE: I'm not.

STEVEN: But you just said –

JOE: I said nothing.

LEN: I don't know what your game is son but it's about time you grew up.

You're on drugs aren't you, what drugs are you on – come on, tell me.

JOE: Tell my mam I'll ring.

Enter VAL.

LEN: I've got work to do.

Exit LEN.

STEVEN: I'll give you a lift to the station.

VAL: You're going.

JOE: Yeah.

STEVEN: I don't know what you want to go for, we've got everything up here now.

VAL: You'll be back for your tea.

STEVEN: Yeah.

Exit STEVEN.

JOE: I have to go.

VAL: You've only just got here.

JOE: I have to go.

VAL: You always have to go.

JOE: I do.

VAL: You never stay.

JOE: I can't, I can't stay – what do you want me to do?

VAL: I don't want you going back to her.

JOE: I'm not.

VAL: What I want, what does it matter what I want.

JOE: Mam.

VAL: You have to go.

JOE: I do.

VAL: Yeah.

JOE: I do.

VAL: You have to go.

JOE: I have to go.

VAL: You're going back to her.

JOE: No, I'm not.

VAL: You'll go back.

JOE: I'm not.

VAL: You'll go back.

JOE: I won't.

VAL: You are.

> *Silence.*

JOE: I can't stay.

VAL: I know.

JOE: I have to go because of work, because of my daughter, because –

VAL: I'll make you up a flask and some sandwiches.

JOE: I haven't got room. I'll get something on the way.

VAL: I'll walk you to the station.

JOE: No. I've got to go, I can't stay – I've got to go, I have to go mam, I have to go – I can't stay.

> *JOE kisses VAL quickly and exits.*

> *VAL sits.*

> *Silence.*

> *VAL opens tobacco tin and takes out the blond lock of hair and turns it between her fingers.*

> *Enter LEN with an accordion.*

> *LEN puts the accordion down.*

LEN: Bloody thing. He's gone then. Bye, he hasn't half got some rubbish up there. I don't know how we'll manage, we'll have to get it all out – we'll have to store it somewhere till they send someone to collect it. Are you alright? Who's going to pay for it all that's what I want to know. They could hardly blame us if we sold the odd bit here and there. Just to cover expenses like. Can I get you anything?

Silence.

VAL: He was beautiful, all yellow and oriental-looking like a Chinaman – they put him in an incubator... poor little thing... sometimes I see him standing beside me just to one side... always in a great big black overcoat – a shock of blond hair – I never see his face... a young man, he would have been – still a youngish man, about –

Crash of pans from the kitchen.

What was that?

LEN: Nothing.

VAL: There's someone in the kitchen.

LEN: There's no one in the kitchen.

What do you want to go bringing all that up for now?

VAL: When I came out the hospital I had nobody, all I had was Joe. I had Joe to look after. They buried him and I don't know where his grave is.

LEN: The baby died and there was nothing anyone could do. It's best forgot.

VAL: I don't know what I would have done if I hadn't had Joe. I wanted to die.

LEN: I sent you money.

VAL: I had nobody.

LEN: I was working, I had to work – I wasn't the father. He walked out I've stayed – out the bloody door at the first sign of trouble – it wasn't my fault, none of it's my fault,

I'm not to blame you can't blame me. It was your life and you made a mess of it – And then there were all the others, you were like a coat hanger ready for any man that could be bothered to pick you up. It's you Shirley gets it from, it's all you.

VAL: I've always wanted to know where his grave is so I can put flowers on it.

Enter SHIRLEY from kitchen.

LEN: It has, it's turned cold.

VAL: I'd like to go for a drive in the country side.

LEN: We haven't got a car.

VAL: You used to have a car.

LEN: Oh yes. I liked having a car. I should have hung onto it, be worth a bob or two now. A Morris Oxford in mint condition would go for thousands now. Leather upholstery and a walnut dashboard. I travelled all over the country in that car, and stopped in hotels. I had a long affair with a barmaid from Chesterfield who loved to drink Martini.

VAL: That's why it finished.

LEN: Yes.

VAL: You like Vodka and Lime.

LEN: At the foot of the mountain.

SHIRLEY: Where's Joe?

VAL: He's gone.

SHIRLEY: He never said goodbye.

SHIRLEY goes to exit.

VAL: Where are you going.

SHIRLEY: Oh, mam.

SHIRLEY puts her arms round VAL and holds her.

SHIRLEY lets go.

Exit SHIRLEY.

LEN: I'll turn the telly on then.

LEN turns on the television.

VAL takes off her shoes.

VAL: We never had proper shoes as children.

LEN: Oh yes, I like this bloke – he can ski backwards and perform amazing dazzling acrobatic tricks in the air.

VAL: I'll start tea then.

Exit VAL.

Silence.

LEN: Hurry up or you'll miss him.

The End